FRAGILE INNOCENCE

FRAGILE INNOCENCE

A Father's Memoir of His Daughter's

Courageous Journey

JAMES RESTON, JR.

HARMONY BOOKS

NEW YORK

Grateful acknowledgment is made to the following for permission to use excerpts from their previously published work:

Excerpt from "The Peace of Wild Things" from Collected Poems: 1957–1982 by Wendell Berry. Copyright © 1985 by Wendell Berry. Reprinted by permission of North Point Press, a division of Farrar, Straus and Giroux, LLC.

Grove/Atlantic, Inc.: Excerpt from *A Personal Matter* by Kenzaburō Ōe. Copyright © 1969 by Grove Press, Inc. Reprinted by permission of Grove/Atlantic, Inc.

Beth Nielsen Chapman: Excerpt from the song lyric "Happy Girl" by Beth Nielsen Chapman/Annie Shoes Roboff. Copyright © 1997 BNC Songs Inc. All rights administered by Almo Music Corp. ASCAP/Almo Music Corp./Anwa Music ASCAP. Reprinted by permission of Beth Nielsen Chapman.

Published in the United States by Harmony Books, an imprint of
the Crown Publishing Group, a division of Random House, Inc., New York.
www.crownpublishing.com

Harmony Books is a registered trademark and the Harmony Books colophon is a trademark of Random House, Inc.

Library of Congress Cataloging-in-Publication Data
Reston, James, 1941–
      Fragile innocence : a father's memoir of his daughter's courageous journey /
James Reston, Jr.—1st ed.
            p. cm.
    1. Reston, Hillary, 1981—Health.   2. Chronically ill children—Biography.
3. Children with disabilities—Biography.   4. Chronically ill children—Family
relationships.   5. Chronically ill children—Care.   I. Title.
    RJ380.R47 2006
    618.92'092—dc22   2005020465

ISBN-13: 978-1-4000-8243-8
ISBN-10: 1-4000-8243-9

Printed in the United States of America

Design by Meryl Sussman Levavi

10   9   8   7   6   5   4   3   2   1

First Edition

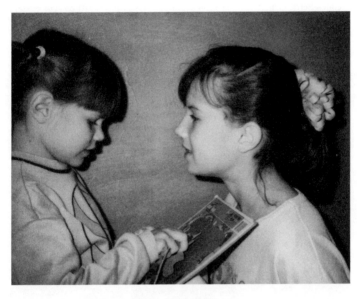

for MAEVE

I have walked and prayed for this young child an hour
And heard the sea-wind scream upon the tower,
And under the arches of the bridge, and scream
In the elms above the flood stream;
Imagining in excited reverie
That the future years had come,
Dancing to a frenzied drum,
Out of the murderous innocence of the sea.

From "A Prayer for My Daughter," by
WILLIAM BUTLER YEATS

———

This is a book about the first twenty-one years of a child named Hillary. It tells of her battle to live and our family's struggle to help her survive as best we could, after an evil and still unidentified force robbed her of her language at age two, hurtled her into a seemingly endless cycle of brain storms, destroyed her kidneys, and took her to the very brink of death. That is the first half of the story, when life itself was at stake.

The second half is different. While the threats to her life never completely vanished, the latter half is about the process of coming to grips with the damage that had been wreaked and the quest to solve the mystery of what had happened. And it is about the heroic efforts of many people, professionals and friends and a few strangers, to help her reach her potential. Ultimately, it is the story of her deliverance and redemption. And so this is memoir, biography, mystery, and drama, all centered in a remarkable person who cannot talk or read or understand language, but who has moved and touched almost everyone she has ever met.

As an innocent devastated by pure chance, Hillary has shown us the very meaning of courage. Without words and frequently with very little physical strength, she has demonstrated a strength of character and an eloquence that many a saint or silver-tongued spellbinder could envy. When the smallest gesture of sensitivity and awareness was shown her, she responded by spreading more love than anyone I have ever known. In Hillary charisma is personified.

The compulsion to write her story has been strong within me for some time. Other writers I admire, among them Reynolds Price, William Styron, Kenzaburō Ōe, and Norman Cousins, have written wonderfully and usefully about grave crises in their personal lives, and so it seemed necessary at some point that I should attempt to do so as well. But the moment had to be right. And the story itself needed some sense of completion. There was never any assurance that Hillary's early life would ever find that resolution, or that we would ever ultimately come to terms with it. But happy events in the summer of 2002 changed that, and completed the circle. Those events, in a far-off and wondrous place called Iowa City, Iowa, allowed me, as it is sometimes said, to close the book.

If I was ready, I could only proceed with the help and sufferance of my wife, Denise Leary. At the most basic level, the mother always suffers and grieves and remembers more than the father. For many of those twenty-one years, I was often the observer high above the fray while Denise, down in the trenches, engaged in the real combat. She had as many or more professional challenges in her career as a lawyer as I have had as a writer. Regardless . . . the mother has no relief, no refuge, no escape. Denise, along with Hillary, is the hero of the story. And to write Hillary's story, I was the observer twice over, for I was the man with the crowbar, as we forced open those misshapen boxes that had long since been closed and put away. For Denise, that was difficult, to say the least.

In the early years of Hillary's illness, we often wondered, angrily, why our child had been singled out, and why we, far from perfect perhaps, but good and decent people, had been cursed. We demanded an answer about the randomness of tragedy. Why us? we asked as if rationality guides the universe. We demanded to comprehend the incomprehensible.

There was precious little to read to impart greater wisdom. And so this book is offered for whatever it may provide to others in similar or worse situations. And the fact is that there are many, many families in far worse situations, families for whom there is no happy ending, no resolution, no redemption. There are many children with far worse infirmities and many families with far fewer advantages than Hillary and we have had. In the Dickensian charnel houses of our own county we have seen scores and scores of them. From these children the common instinct is to avert one's eyes. In Hillary's imperfections, by contrast to other families, we have been blessed. To those families and to those children, we offer our love and admiration, and our hope that by reading this they may find some profit.

Not everything about Hillary's life is told herein. Certain confidences are protected. That so much could be told is a factor of Hillary's own situation. I have not invaded her privacy, nor undermined her dignity as a human being, for she lives in the moment, on the evidence of her eyes about what transpires before her. She is an innocent, without embarrassment or guilt or remorse or resentment. I like to think that she would be pleased to have her story told.

Beyond its human qualities, her story should be told for an additional reason, one that I came to realize only gradually over the years. Her case personalizes some of the most daunting ethical issues of medicine that face us today: stem cell research, animal organ transplantation, the politics of human organ donation, genetic manipulation, diagnosis with the human genome map, and reproductive and therapeutic cloning. These issues are seldom considered from the vantage point of the "consumer." Hillary is a potential consumer—and beneficiary—of it all.

We sit now by a favorite stream in the Blue Ridge. She plies her joyous pastime of throwing sticks into the spring-swollen water of Fiery Run, turning to smile and squint her pleasure at me. To my eyes, she is lovely, and the scene is worthy of Wyeth. Her throaty, tremulous sounds are loud, but their loudness does not offend the countryside. Their warble reminds me of a distant night heron in the far woods. Healthy and solid at last, rosy-cheeked and bright-eyed, her life force is evident. She is making up for lost time.

FIERY RUN, VIRGINIA

MAY 2005

FRAGILE INNOCENCE

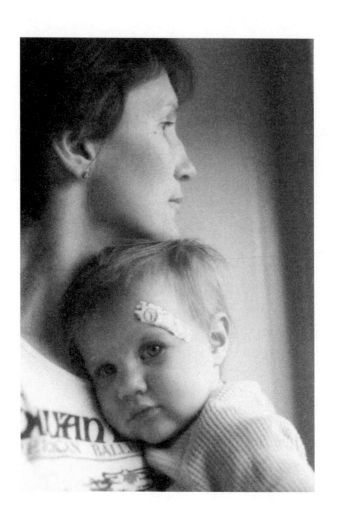

Part I

LIFE ITSELF

CHAPTER ONE

———

[1]

The year 1981 was the end of an era in our personal lives. But we did not know yet that a much-longer, more-complicated era was about to begin. For ten years, from the moment I married that willowy, tough-minded, high-spirited, and high-cheekboned girl from the Bronx in a retrograde ceremony in the Blue Ridge Mountains, we had lived the often ecstatic, sometimes stormy, perfectly ordinary existence of two young lovers trying to solidify our union as we started our careers and our family outside Chapel Hill, North Carolina. In that decade I had published five books, two of them novels, launched my first play, and taught creative writing at the University of

North Carolina. At the end of the decade, we had two children: Maeve, who arrived in 1978 as the envy of the Gerber baby advertisers, and then Devin, who came floppy-eared in 1980, as the fastest crawler in the East.

Denise is seven years my younger. In the twilight of late sixties activism we met in New York City, where together we worked in the spirit of the times at a poverty program called the Neighborhood Youth Corps. The program was run by one of Mayor John Lindsay's most controversial associates, Rabbi Sam Schrage. A stocky, rotund man of Brazilian extraction, he was the community leader in Crown Heights, a tense neighborhood deep in Brooklyn, evenly split between Jews and blacks. Amid the ravages of constant street battles in Crown Heights, he had organized the Maccabees, a private defense force for the Jewish community, and thus he was a polarizing figure for blacks.

For us, however, he was a shadchan. In his matchmaking he was persistent and effective, and after we were engaged, we asked him to marry us. In sorrow and in self-interest he declined. It would never do for our marriage to appear in the *New York Times,* he said, with controversial Rabbi Schrage as the officiate. We were Christian. For him to tie our knot would destroy his standing in his community. But he would come to our ceremony, he promised, even if it was to be held in the terrifying darkness of rural Virginia, so long as he could get there before sundown on Friday.

In our first years in North Carolina, Denise completed

her law degree at Duke and received her basic training in the dusty, elemental courtrooms of the rural South. Late in the 1970s she reconnected with her great mentor, Chuck Morgan, the powerful and brilliant Alabamian who had been run out of Birmingham for his passionate criticism of the local establishment after the bombing of the Sixteenth Street Baptist Church and had gone on to be such a champion of civil rights. Chuck had made it possible for Denise to hold on to her profession by her fingernails, by doing research projects and writing briefs from home, while she concentrated on the needs of her children.

But Denise, raised in a small apartment in the northeast Bronx and educated in Boston, was by nature a big-city girl. She had never been to the South when I dragged her there, by way of Berea, Kentucky, in our first year of married life. She had never really taken to the place. The South of 1971 still had ugly vestiges of racism, as well as blind patriotism in the face of Vietnam outrages, and a sexism that treated "the little lady from up North" with undisguised contempt. In her law school class she was one of 28 women in a class of 120. The idealism of the 1960s still influenced most of the class, men and women, and this majority saw the law as a way to further civil rights and to harness corporate greed in the spirit of Teddy Roosevelt's trustbusters. But a growing contingent was made up of pasty yuppies with ten-day haircuts and briefcases, with their eye on Wall Street and corporate America. This group was epitomized by a pudgy, walleyed nerd from Illinois named Ken Starr.

Southern racism and chauvinism offended Denise viscerally, as they did me. But I was more involved with the pleasures and amusements of Southern living, partly because I had been partaking of them a lot longer. By 1981 I had spent fourteen years in the South, the bulk of my adult life up until that time, and considered myself, at least in part, an adoptive Southerner. Inevitably, when I came north, my friends remarked upon the soft Southern lilt that had invaded my speech over those years. As a college student at UNC, I had been through the heady desegregation struggles of the early sixties, and so I knew what raw, open, sanctioned racism was like and had witnessed the remarkable changes.

After my three years in the Army (1965–68), I had entered the vibrant literary scene of North Carolina, the scene dominated by a handsome, vigorous, upright, and wickedly funny Reynolds Price and festooned with Lee Smith, Doris Betts, and, later, a young Allan Gurganus with hair. In the South of their birth, of course, they had found much that was touching and funny. As an outsider, I had often enjoyed jolly times with them, as they spun their tales about the eccentric characters of their youth. But my roots were in Washington, in privilege and plenty, the scion of a famous journalist and a beautiful, vivacious mother. My childhood characters were politicians and power brokers and tough-talking, hard-drinking newsmen. The Ivy League had seemed my natural course, but a wonderful scholarship had lured me south, and with it I became part of the region's inevitable dilution.

I had no interest in becoming a "Southern writer." Destined forever to be an outsider, that was the way I preferred it. But I loved the wit and lore of these superior writers, and was never able quite to replicate their bonhomie when I left the South. In that transitional decade between Johnson and Reagan, even the hulking ghost of Thomas Wolfe lingered in the shadows, however indistinctly. I could still thrill to its presence, and it pleased me to premiere my first play on the very boards of the Old Playmakers Theatre, where Wolfe had performed as a student actor in the 1920s.

My view of Dixie was thus more textured than Denise's. Courthouse louts rather than literati populated her early lawyer's life. It was harder for her to find humor in the South's idiosyncrasies.

The year 1981 saw the publication of the hardest book I ever wrote, or ever would write: my narrative of the Jonestown mass suicide in Guyana in 1978. To be good, a book must be the product of an author's obsession, where a subject grabs him like a pit bull and never lets go until the last page proof is polished. For me Jonestown had been a three-year obsession. Its challenge was to comprehend the incomprehensible, to imagine the unimaginable, and to write about it without resorting to cant. The story was horrible, even soul-withering, but it was also utterly fascinating.

Both literary and political impulses drew me to it. Its parallel to Conrad's *Heart of Darkness* was obvious, but here was life imitating and even improving upon art. To me Jones was a bolder, larger, more compelling figure than Kurtz, and a more terrifying one. He was real, and he was an American monster, of my age, and ironically with some of my same passions. In the story I saw the possibility of making tangible what Conrad could only imagine.

But the politics and the psychology behind the story drew me to the saga as much as its literary connection. How could this madman, Jim Jones, have lured so many bright and well-intentioned young people like myself into his web, using the very same arguments about racial harmony and antimilitarism that moved me? And why had they not bolted instead of bowing down when they watched Jones go mad before their very eyes? In this grisly tale lay the eternal question about the moment of disobedience in the face of crime and immorality. There was plenty in the Jonestown story to sustain a three-year obsession. As it turned out, the obsession lasted a few years longer than that, as I dealt with the material first in a book, then in a radio documentary, then in a play, and finally in a libretto for an opera.

But the effort exhausted me physically and emotionally, and, apart from my dark moods that strained my young marriage, it had brought me to the brink of madness. Later I would come to know that other Jonestown veterans had gone off the deep end. There was something about the story that got inside one's head and gravitated to that part of the brain where the wiring is weak and subject to short circuit. One reporter, I learned, had stopped over in Barbados after leaving Guyana and took a room in a beachside tower hotel on the fourteenth floor. During the night, he had moved all the furniture in the room against the door to blockade Jones's nightmare goons, whom he imagined to be outside his door and about to break in on him. That reporter never recovered from the experience.

I had flown to Guyana five days after the mass suicide. Shortly afterward, as the only pure author in a planeload of war-hardened newsmen such as Peter Arnett, I helicoptered into Jonestown after the Guyanese army and the FBI had taken out the last body bag.

That the bodies were gone made the scene more terrifying, for one had to imagine how it had been only a few short days before. Around the buildings they had plowed a swathe as if it were some jacklegged cordon sanitaire. If I was the only author there, I was also a new father, for Maeve was then ten months old. Outside the plowed perimeter, I walked in tall grass, and came upon the discarded potties and milk bottles and toddler toys of dead children . . . and quietly went insane.

A few days later when I landed in Chapel Hill and swept Maeve up into my arms, I knew I was in serious trouble. And so I rushed to North Carolina Memorial Hospital and barged into the office of the only psychiatrist I knew in those days. Before the wise and accomplished Dr. Maury Lipton, I broke down in a total collapse. About that first session, in which he saved my sanity, I remember best the oranges on his desk, which he made me peel slowly as I blubbered on and on about my horror and my confusion. Eventually he talked me through my "panic attack."

In the subsequent three years, I would consult with Maury Lipton occasionally as I tried to make sense of Jonestown. But never were those other sessions as dangerous as that first one.

In March 1981, at our twenty-two-acre farm named Monarch Glade—named for the monarch butterflies that flooded the place in September, and its secluded, pine-surrounded field off the road—I finally opened the box that contained my author copies of *Our Father Who Art in Hell: The Life and Death of Jim Jones.* That dark journey through my own madness and the madness of a thousand others was finally over, I thought. And in opening that box I made a promise to myself: never again would I write about so difficult and depressing a subject.

Somehow the act of both opening that box and shutting it at the same time called for us to do something big, something life-affirming, in our personal life. How could we go on as before, after this? At last, after ten years of using every defense from yammering to four corners, I gave in to Denise's full-court press to leave North Carolina for her beloved New York City. I regarded my offer as temporary, perhaps a year or two, before we would return, city-hardened and big-time-connected, to Monarch Glade. I did not easily leave our eccentric Japanese house, which we had designed together with our tobacco-chomping architect, or the separate study way down the field all for me. Somehow I knew that I would never again have so perfect a writer's circumstance. Chapel Hill was supposed to be Blue Heaven. I should have known that once Denise got me out of the South, she was never going back.

Pulling up stakes for New York was a big step and may even have been profound, but it was not exactly life-affirming—not, at least, in the sense of providing an antidote to Jim Jones's death wishes. For that department we left things to chance and surprise. And as chance would have it, Denise's father was coming down to our tiny, open Japanese house, with its loft arrangement where we slept in a bed I had made from old eaves and plywood. The house had only one door you could close for privacy, and that had become the room of our two toddlers. Her father would be sleeping in the foldout couch below our loft. Denise made her calculations.

Math was never her strong suit. And so in those few days when the tree frogs began their peeping in the nearby bog and the whippoorwill could be heard deep in the night, Hillary was conceived.

[2]

We learned on tax day. By Denise's memory we had characteristically opposite reactions. She was overwhelmed at the idea not just of having a third child on our modest budget, which was already stretched to the maximum, but a third child so close in age to the other two. This sensible reaction brought her close to tears. I, by contrast, broke out into hysterical laughter at the news, and had to be calmed down some minutes later before I received a punch in the nose.

In mid-July we left Chapel Hill for New York. For a month, with a grand vista of the Hudson River, we camped out in the commodious apartment of William Sloane Coffin, who had graciously offered his place to us while he was on vacation from his job as senior minister at Riverside Church. I was Reverend Coffin's longtime fan. I admired his activism in civil rights and his opposition to the Vietnam War, and I had spent a wonderful evening with him a few years before at Yale when he was still chaplain there. His living room was full of boisterous, fun-loving students, and the evening was replete with laughter, good conversation, games, and music, with Coffin himself holding forth forcefully on the piano. We had a strange bond. As I had been a military intelligence officer in the Army, he had been in the CIA before he went into the ministry. It was evident from our talks that in some deep emotional sense he thought of his ministry as a compensation for whatever dire things he may have done as a spook.

A year and a half later, I learned something very different from Coffin. On a cold and stormy Monday morning in January 1983, his son Alex skidded off the road and plunged to his death in Boston Harbor. The following Sunday I was in the congregation when Coffin preached his extraordinary sermon. Riverside Church was packed with hundreds of his friends and admirers who had come to be with him in tragedy. To my amazement, but not surprise, Reverend Coffin ascended the pulpit with strength and grace. His booming voice was unwavering, and his message had wisdom and strange anger and even a touch of humor.

"My twenty-four-year-old son, Alexander," he began, "who enjoyed beating his old man at every game and in every race, beat his father to the grave."

His anger that day was not directed at the Fates, but at a good-hearted woman who, in trying to console him a few days before in his sister's parlor, had said, "I just don't understand the will of God." Coffin had turned on her with his full wrath, and because he was so large a man physically, his aspect must have been awesome. "Nothing so infuriates me as the incapacity of seemingly intelligent people to get it through their heads that God doesn't go around this world with his finger on triggers, his fist around knives, his hands on steering wheels," the grieving man told his grieving congregation. "God is dead set against all unnatural deaths . . . The one thing that should never be said when someone dies is 'it is the will of God.' Never do we know enough to say that. My own consolation lies in knowing that it is not the will of God that Alex die; that when the waves closed over the sinking car, God's heart was the first of all our hearts to break."

He closed with a verse from Emily Dickinson:

> By a departing light
> We see acuter quite
> Than by a wick that stays.

There's something in the flight
That clarifies the sight
And decks the rays.

From time to time over the past twenty years, Coffin's sermon has fleeted into my mind. Did I really believe him? That in suffering and tragedy there was no hand of God, and that in unnecessary suffering, particularly of children, God's heart is the first to break? We could not be so accepting. If there is a God, Coffin's permissive attitude seemed to let him off the hook. At least in Hillary's early years, we stood more with the woman in the parlor than with Coffin.

His text that day had been from Romans 8:38–39: "For I am persuaded that neither death, nor life, nor angels, nor principalities, nor powers, nor things present, nor things to come, nor height, nor depth, nor any other creature, shall be able to separate us from the love of God, which is in Christ Jesus our Lord."

We were not so persuaded as he.

In late summer we found our new nest on the loveliest street in Brooklyn. We were, of course, not the first to discover this special one-block street called Montgomery Place in Park Slope. In fact, its classic, turn-of-the-century, ivy-covered brownstones occasionally became the set for expensive television commercials. Within a few weeks of our arrival, the street was blocked off by the police so that an actress in a coffee commercial could pop her head out of a second-story window, in what seemed like a hundred takes, to shout, "Coffee's ready!"

We took charge of the upper two floors of a house whose lower floors were retained by the owner, an art dealer named Robert Israel. When Devin, then moving toward his terrible twos, would jump boisterously on the floor, we would caution him about jumping on Mrs. Israel's head.

Like every parent of previous children, we had our rituals about childbirth. Devin had arrived in the wake of a particularly spicy Mexican meal at a Chapel Hill joint known as Tijuana Fats. And labor for our firstborn, Maeve, began while Denise was trying to balance a conversation with the head of Alan Dershowitz's legal team in a first amendment case with the preparation of French pastry. That would be the last time she ever made Gâteau Pithivier, or mixed law and pastry. But this pregnancy would have a different connection. In the unhealthy air of New York, Denise had developed a fierce case of bronchitis. Between her hacking cough and her hoisting of her children, she cracked two ribs. This made her quite a sight at the old Association of the Bar of the City of New York library, where she labored for Chuck Morgan. Apart from her difficulties in moving the chair close enough to the table to write, she had her left arm in a sling. Such a constriction was, of course, hard for me to imagine. As usual I was not the most sympathetic type. We joked about hitting a particularly deep pothole on the FDR Drive on the rush to New York Hospital when the time came. Sure enough, we hit it hard late on November 30, and Hillary popped into the world an hour and a half later. That the Reston family would be launched by potholes, enchiladas, and rough puff pastry seemed somehow to harbinger what lay ahead.

The births of our first two children in the local county hospital in North Carolina had been handled with sensitivity, in home-birthing rooms appointed with living-room furniture, and shepherded by sensitive doctors with delicate hands. My most traumatic experience had been to witness Devin's circumcision. In the children's infancy the care had been equally good, under Dr. Terry Fry, whom our Maeve had renamed Dr. French Fry.

Now we were going to learn how New York handled birth: the South Asian residents were supercilious, the nurses screamed at the doctors, and "our" doctor refused to turn up until the absolute last second. Then his first minutes in the hospital were spent on the hallway telephone discussing personal business, presumably with his wife. Only after the nurse shouted coarsely to him from the labor room, "You better get in here!" did he focus on the birth of Hillary.

By then Hillary was already birthing herself. The only saving grace of this disheartening experience was that Denise avoided the cold stirrups and glaring lights of the sterile hospital delivery room, of which she had a particular dread.

These slights and disappointments faded quickly with the sweet smell of vernix, the feel of the downy head, the sounds of a dove, and, eventually, the results of the PKU test, which revealed nothing out of the ordinary. I turned up the next day with a bouquet of roses, the kind that glisten along the avenue in the late afternoon and keel over in the next morning's light.

We were back in Brooklyn in a day, and a week later Hillary received her second bouquet. It came with a note and a poem from Maryssa Gilbride, Denise's best friend from law school, who possesses a round, freckled face and an eternally merry disposition. They had bonded in their Irishness, and we had officially declared Maryssa to be the "tante" of our children. To Hillary, she wrote that "based upon your siblings, beauty is inevitable, but knowing the character of your mother and father, I take courage that you will learn to handle it gracefully." To that bouquet she pinned a Yeats poem, written in June 1919 and titled "A Prayer for My Daughter." Maryssa had written out its many verses in her own graceful hand, and retitled it "A Prayer for Their Daughter—Denise and Jim," signed it "Your devoted tante." The poem put forward a concept of "radical innocence," a concept that might well stand for Hillary's entire life, and among its verses was this:

> *May she become a flourishing hidden tree*
> *That all her thoughts may like the linnet be,*
> *And have no business but dispensing round*
> *Their magnanimities of sound,*
> *Nor but in merriment begin a chase,*
> *Nor but in merriment a quarrel.*

O may she live like some green laurel
Rooted in one dear perpetual place.

And so it was to be: Her innocence was to be radical; her thoughts and sounds were to be like those of a finch; and she was to be rooted in a dear perpetual place.

[3]

Eighteen is a robust, cardinal number, associated with big trucks and powerful artillery shells, large barrels and fast schooners, the century of Enlightenment and the daunting Prohibition of the Eighteenth Amendment. Eighteen years is the time for coming of age, the time to vote and to drink alcohol and to break away. In the case of our Hillary, eighteen months as well as eighteen years marked an important passage.

In those first eighteen months of her life, we settled into our new life in the city. Brooklyn's delights were all nearby. We frolicked almost daily in the rolling contours of Prospect Park, took in shows at the Brooklyn Museum, delighted in the sea turtles and beluga whales at the Brooklyn Aquarium, strolled through Grand Army Plaza and thought of its arch as the Brandenburg Gate. We were often at the botanical garden, especially in our first spring in Brooklyn when the cherry blossoms were out in the Japanese garden. We would push Hillary's grand baby carriage beneath the blizzard of falling petals. Denise would reach down into the stroller and switch on a tape recording of the hummingbird chorus in *Madama Butterfly*. (I liked to think of myself as the "Yankee vagabondo" of the piece.) We rode the D train to Manhattan so often, to take in Denise's old childhood haunts, that the rivets and pillars of the Manhattan Bridge became as familiar as every pine tree had been on our endless car trips between North Carolina and Washington.

Brooklyn's Seventh Avenue was our commercial street. In those days before virulent gentrification, it was still a thoroughfare of delis and butchers, cleaners and candy stores. At Seventh Avenue and Fourth Street was the "hiccup truck" store, as Devin called it, for he was then heavily into cars and trucks. Pickup trucks were his favorite. When the garbage men came early in the morning, clattering and throwing the metal garbage cans around and shouting at one another noisily below us, we heard one shout to his mate one morning, "Hey, Joe! Over here and help with this one." Forever after, we were on the lookout for "Garbage Truck Joe." When we moved to Washington later and became more cosmopolitan (and after we watched Charlie Chaplin's *Great Dictator*), Garbage Truck Joe became Herr Garbich.

That first winter brought the worst blizzard in New York memory. For two weeks the temperature plunged into single digits; the winds were sub-hurricane strength, and several snowfalls on successive days dropped twenty-four inches of snow. With the wind and the work of the snowplows—one of them undoubtedly driven by Joe—the pileup was far greater, until along Eighth Avenue, the snowbanks came to the bottom branches of the curbside trees. On the radio were terrible reports of people freezing, and of a plane crash in Washington—an Air Florida jet that had not been properly deiced had hit the Fourteenth Street Bridge and plunged into the Potomac.

Finally, the pileup in our neighborhood was so great that Eighth Avenue was closed to traffic. Brooklyn became a magical winter carnival. Jolly crowds strolled their carless avenues with a great sense of sport. We had returned, however briefly, to the horse-and-carriage days of Teddy Roosevelt and experienced its smogless pleasures. In our snug bastion we turned out all the lights and cuddled by the window so we could watch the waves of snow swirl around the street light below. Life was good.

That winter Maeve settled into kindergarten at the Berkeley Carroll School, and Devin attended preschool at the Temple Beth Emmanuel School around the corner, where he learned to sing "I had a little dreidel" and to venerate the menorah. Hillary, meanwhile, developed normally, taking well to her rocking cradle, where she slept with one arm on her chest, Napoleon-like, a harbinger of many imperial dictates that were to come. She was, according to her doctor's notes, alert, active, and social, a baby who laughed a lot and had good hand-mouth coordination. True, she had her quota of ear infections and colds, and she suffered from a hellish colic. It forced her onto a special diet, anchored by a powder called Pregestimil that we, with our 1960s reference points and our hard-pressed budget, referred to as Acapulco Gold because it cost $13 a can. The doctor's notes from her one-year checkup in December 1982 referred to her status: she stood alone, walked holding on, and spoke, usually a hearty "ma-ma," "da-da," and "ba-ba."

That our children were highly verbal was a special source of pride. To encourage this quality I began to write poetry with the children during our second winter in Brooklyn. After dinner we would repair to my fourth floor, roof-line study. With a child on each knee and Hillary close by on a shag rug, we would bang them out on my 1938 Royal typewriter: poems about sensitive dinosaurs or Maeve's favorite planet, Pluto, about magic tricks or Maeve's friend Handles Clark. Handles Clark was rich material, for she had limpid blue eyes and pretty blond hair braided into loops that reminded you of the handles on the old L train. We wrote about Devin's puckered-up gurami fish and about many wondrous adventures with his bunnies, for he never went anywhere without them. Each kid took on a persona. Maeve was Rainbow O'Leary, bespeaking her interest in all things flouncy and colorful; Devin was Ice because he was so cool; and for her bombast, Hillary was Fireworks. And so the poem "Ice, Fireworks, and Rainbow O'Leary."

> *Ice is a little, blond haired boy*
> *Who always makes a kissing gurami face*
> *and shouts "It's not fair."*
>
> *Fireworks is a little English baby*
> *Her brother, Ice, taught her how to scream.*

When someone has a toy she wants, she screams.
And after she screams, she gets the toy.

Rainbow O'Leary is five years old, a brunette.
She is in kindergarten. Her brother, Ice, is always
under her feet.
She loves her brother, and her little sister, Fireworks.

One day, Ice, Fireworks, and Rainbow O'Leary
went to the Aquarium.
There, they saw sparkling, pretty rainbow fish
And a stingray tried to eat a lionfish,
But the lionfish sprayed its poison out of its tentacles
And killed the stingray.
And Ice, Fireworks, and Rainbow thought the
lionfish was clever.

As Hillary moved into her second year, it seemed that she would be the most verbal of the three. Her language began with her interest in the finches that inhabited the bird feeder on our balcony, and so *birdy* was her second word after, of course, *daddy.* Before long her vocabulary was well ahead of her peers'. If she was verbal, she was also lively, sociable, and dramatic. She had a particularly stagey way of entering a room where she would appear, throw one arm out to her fans while the other hand clutched her heart, and announce herself, in the best Tallulah Bankhead manner: "Doll-baby, oooi, oooi, oh!" Because I was working on a play at the time, this theatrical bent pleased me immensely. But the sound "oooi, oooi, oh!" became the code for the happy, bright, theatrical, sociable personality that was Hillary.

Being in New York had provided an instant jolt to my standing as a writer. The phone was ringing with calls from publishers and agents and magazine editors as it never had done in my perfect study back at Monarch Glade. And a good thing it was, too. The wolf was always at the door, and I was keenly aware of the six eyes trained on me from below for the next meal. Furiously, I wrote for *The New Yorker, Esquire, The New York Times Magazine, Omni.* I was working on a stage adaptation of my Jim Jones book in Providence, Rhode Island, with an iconoclastic and brilliant director, Adrian Hall. We were searching, I breezily told the *Providence Journal,* for the "emotional truth" of Jonestown. During that patch I did my first film for PBS, *88 Seconds in Greensboro,* about an agent provacateur named Eddie Dawson who had guided a Ku Klux Klan caravan to a protest of civil rights workers in Greensboro, North Carolina, where shooting broke out and three protesters were murdered. And *The New Yorker* had paid me the astronomical sum of $20,000 to retrace General William Tecumseh Sherman's march through the South. When my publisher heard about it, he offered a somewhat more earthbound sum of $12,000 to expand the *New Yorker* piece to book length.

But no matter how smoothly and efficiently I folded one magazine piece on top of another or spiced the work with a book project and the theater and television, it was never good enough. There was never enough money. Besides the fact that I was constantly on the road, we were going seriously into debt after our second year in New York, and I began to think about bailing out of the big city.

In the spring of 1983, we told Mr. Israel that we were leaving. No doubt Mrs. Israel and her head could at last sense some relief.

Hillary was approaching her eighteenth month of life.

CHAPTER TWO

---

[1]

In May 1983 Devin and I packed up, and took off for Virginia, hauling the first load of the family belongings. For our transition to some still-undefined yet more-permanent and less-expensive location, the family was headed for the Blue Ridge Mountains.

In his columns in the *New York Times,* my father had made our country retreat into a mythical place of cool breezes and quiet contemplation. About sixty miles outside of Washington, it lies along a hilly, narrow road in Fauquier County that was gravel when we first traveled it, and he went there to reflect at a distance about the dizzying swirl of Washington politics. His byline, Fiery Run,

Virginia, was much beloved by his readers, for it often presaged a spoof on the stupidity of city folk or the transience of windy officeholders or the exorbitant cost of creating a tomato garden or the kindliness of country neighbors.

In fact there is a stream called Fiery Run. It flows from the heights of Rattlesnake Mountain to the north, down a narrow valley, and past our pasture, which makes up the "lower forty" of our expansive, eleven-acre spread. Across the stream the Mill House stands proudly, in judgment and in decline, and in memory of when in the nineteenth century this was the neighborhood gathering place for grain and gossip. In the 1860s the gossip was particularly juicy there, since according to local lore the miller, Robert Sims, was Jesse James's father-in-law. The infamous Rutherford brothers who rode with Jesse grew up just over the hill, just as Robert Ford, a mean little boy by all accounts, was raised up the road before, as a man, he shot Jesse James in the back in Kansas. The bandit's demise was not to the liking of our miller, who immediately hit the road for Kansas and extracted honorable revenge on mean little Robert Ford.

Now only the miller's house remains by the stream, next to the ruin of his mill itself, which I always believed my dad had burned down by leaving a smoldering pipe on a nearby stump. Over the stream is a one-lane bridge, which he bought from the State of Virginia for a dollar when its engineers announced they were going to tear the relic down to make way for a two-laner. Eventually Fiery

Run flows into the Rappahannock River, and is forgotten, but we remember it, for its rocks, and its cattle guards, and its coolness on a hot summer day.

Many have envied this place. It is an enclave surrounded by the five-thousand-acre ranch of the hotel magnate William Marriott. No structures are within sight except for the twelve-room brick house built in 1812 by the brother of Chief Justice John Marshall and the far-off barns of Fairfield Farm. There, as a kid, I mounted the lumbering workhorses and rode the manure spreaders with the black hands and watched old Mr. Price birth the lambs in January. In those days Fairfield was owned by a Belgian countess named Baroness Jeanne von Reininghauf Lambert. The baroness was a Rothschild and a principal owner of the Bank of Belgium, a romantic figure altogether whose husband had been seized by the Nazis at the beginning of World War II, and who lived in exile in the Blue Ridge until 1949. Despite her down-to-earth manner, great mystery hovered around this exotic aristocrat. It was whispered that she had brought bricks of gold bullion with her from Belgium. But where along Fiery Run had she stashed them?

My folks had restored the modest cabin on the bluff overlooking the stream and had purchased another cabin, which was brought log by log and attached to the original, so that the house is L-shaped, with a flagstone porch in its crevice. There we spent countless evenings throughout my childhood watching the sun set over Mount Marshall and once killing a water moccasin that had strayed up from the stream. My most vivid memory of the early days is taking the honey bucket down to the lime pit, since we had no running water.

If the mill was mythical for my father, it was magical for me. In a special way it melded life, love, and work. My parents had purchased it in 1948 for $5,000 soon after I had nearly been killed on a Georgetown street. Then a wispy seven-year-old, with only the city streets to entertain me, I had been socked between the eyes by a softball that had been fouled off as I stood behind the catcher at a pickup softball game in Georgetown Park. I had turned, bawling, and stepped foursquare onto Q Street and in front of a city bus, which ran me over and fractured my skull. I can remember to this day the fleeting moment I opened my eyes in the backseat of that generous motorist who had scraped me off the pavement and whisked me to the emergency room of the old Georgetown Hospital. My parents were haunted by guilt at being away, but it was in the nature of our lives. Restons are always away, it seems, at times of tragedy. But we got Fiery Run out of the deal, so it wasn't a total loss.

Many years later, after my stint in the Army, I had returned to this refuge of workhorses and manure spreaders and snakes and kindly neighbors to live alone and write. That was during the fall of 1968, when I came to finish my first novel, and to expunge, through literary labor, my ambivalence about my dutiful military service in an immoral enterprise.

Three years later Denise and I had been married on

the cabin's expansive lawn. She had worn a lovely white dress purchased at Bergdorf Goodman, for at heart she is a traditionalist. But her bridesmaids, largely at my insistence, had worn long green paisley skirts and white peasant tops. Radical that I was (in my head), I presented myself in a white turtleneck, blue bell-bottom trousers, and a lei of white gardenias around my neck.

Typical of the time, we had written our own marriage ceremony. It was full of poetry and rebellion and intense feeling. Once our friends were gathered on the soggy lawn—the ceremony had to be delayed three hours because of rain—I read to Denise John Donne's "Love's Growth" with its opening lines "I scarce believe my love to be so pure / As I had thought it was / Because it doth endure / Vicissitude, and season, as the grass . . ." And she had responded with e. e. cummings: "be unto love as rain is unto color; create me gradually (for as these emerging now hills invent the air) / my trembling where my still unvisible when. wait if i am not heart, because at least i beat . . ."

And Rabbi Schrage had read, in his booming, wonderfully accented voice, from the evocative, sensual passages of the Song of Solomon: "Set me as a seal upon thine heart, as a seal upon thine arm; for love is strong as death; jealousy is cruel as the grave; the coals thereof are coals of fire, which hath a most vehement flame. Many waters cannot quench love, neither can the floods drown it; if a man would give all the substance of his house for love, it would utterly be contemned."

In the spirit of Solomon we danced to the country music of the Virginia Gentlemen amid hay bales and the flower arrangements and old friends before we raced off to our wedding night at the Red Fox Tavern in Middleburg, and Denise spread the petals of my gardenia lei on the big four-poster bed.

In the coming week, as we honeymooned giddily in New Orleans, I came to realize that our wedding had had a significant subplot. As we were exchanging vows in Virginia, the *New York Times* was preparing to publish the first installment of the Pentagon Papers. My father had been intimately involved in the secret process of preparing this Olympian scoop, and no doubt his mind was as much on the next day's paper as on his second son's marriage. As the gathering waited for the rain to stop and crowded into our simple living room at the cabin, my father had whispered the news to his old friend Katharine Graham.

It must have been a form of torture for her. Under the circumstances she could scarcely seize the telephone and pass on the news to her colleagues at the *Washington Post*. In her memoir, *Personal History*, Kay Graham mentions our "casual wedding" as the place she heard about the Pentagon Papers. But ever the lady, she did not write of her irritation at how long this infernal wedding was taking.

We were oblivious to this undercurrent. We flew off blissfully to New Orleans for our honeymoon, unaware and indifferent to anything we could not see more than a few feet from our faces . . . and touch. And my annoying father insisted on interrupting our activities every day with a phone call to our humid guesthouse in the Big Easy about the latest news from big-time journalism.

A day after our arrival in Virginia, Denise called from New York to report that Hillary was running a very high fever and was vomiting. As upsetting as this was, we had experienced the same condition with the other children, and, on that first night, we were not overly alarmed. Denise had talked with the pediatrician, Dr. Esther Silverman, and she had dispensed the usual bromide. The condition was probably viral. Denise was to alternate aspirin and Tylenol every two hours and to soak Hillary in cool baths. If the temperature was not down in the morning, she should come in.

It was not down in the morning. Indeed, the temperature was spiking at 104 degrees, and Hillary was listless. And so they piled in a cab for the $40 round-trip to Manhattan and to Dr. Silverman's Park Avenue office. Dr. Silverman was a cheerful, bright, exacting young doctor who had just opened her practice. Because she had just had her own second child and dressed with flair, she connected comfortably with young upscale mothers. She explained illness well in her lyrical European accent, and parents went away reassured that their children were in good capable hands, even if the wait in a packed sitting room sometimes felt like being in an airplane stacked up over La Guardia. When we left her office, our conversations often ended benignly with remarks about the color of shoes that Dr. Silverman had worn on that particular day, for the color was never the same.

After an examination Dr. Silverman stuck to her original view. With no evidence of bacterial infection, with a test for meningitis negative, this must be some unspecified viral infection, for which there was no precise remedy. Denise trudged home with the same instructions about pain relievers, cool baths, clear liquids, and to call in the morning if there was no change. The next day, a Saturday, brought no change: same temperature, same trip to Park Avenue, same instructions. The doctor's notes had the air of contradiction: "Persistent temp. spikes to 104–105 degrees yesterday. Today started mild diarrhea. P.E. No new findings from previous visit. Essentially unremarkable exam." If the visit was unremarkable for Dr. Silverman, Denise was becoming frantic and more assertive. Fine, Dr. Silverman replied. If the fever is not down overnight, Hillary should go to the emergency room at Lenox Hill Hospital.

What we now know is that these were critical hours in Hillary's life. They were pivotal, profound, life-altering. Without anybody knowing it, she was teetering on the knife's edge. Her tiny body was under fierce attack. A secret, aggressive, evil seed had planted itself in her brain, and as each day of innocuous aspirins and cool baths passed without it being discovered and isolated, it wrought havoc.

The following day, a rainy Sunday, the quality of Hillary's lethargy was terrifying, and Denise rushed her to

Lenox Hill Hospital in desperation. There, somewhere down a sterile hallway, shunted off to the side, far from the main emergency room, where the victims of a New York Saturday night with more obvious problems were rushed by on stretchers, Hillary was again seen, this time by a young resident who dismissed her four days of continuous spiking, rolling temperatures as unremarkable. Diagnosis: viral syndrome. Treatment recommended: Tylenol.

"How do you know this won't come back to haunt her?" Denise said coldly to the resident.

On the fifth day the temperature finally broke. Several weeks later, just before we left New York for good, Hillary returned to Dr. Silverman's office for her eighteen-month checkup.

"Mother reports child is back to baseline," the medical record announced flatly. But the baseline was more like sand beneath us, shifting and drifting and soon to wash us out to sea.

[2]

Through the summer of 1983 I was often away, as usual. My focus was the stage adaptation of my Jonestown book in Providence. The director, Adrian Hall, was fast becoming a unique and important presence in my life; I was flattered to be working with such a towering figure in the theatrical world and wanted to make the most of the experience. Over the years he had worked with the great ones— Lillian Hellman, Robert Penn Warren, Harold Pinter, and Tennessee Williams—and had refused to work with

William Styron on a play Adrian felt was ill-conceived. In Providence his Trinity Square Repertory Company was at the forefront of the regional theater "movement," of which Adrian himself was a passionate leader. At core, his theatrical philosophy was the "confrontation" between the actors and the audience, and this had led him to a number of controversial productions with difficult material, including a play of which he was particularly proud about Charles Manson. The company of resident actors had won a Tony Award for its work, largely because so many actors loved Adrian, and forsook Broadway and the commercial theater in New York to be near him.

In such heady company humdrum matters like child rearing and family finances could not divert me. At Fiery Run Denise did her best to contain her resentments. She missed New York and thought she'd succeeded in getting us out of the South for good, only to find herself once again in crackerland, in a cabin with the scent of mice and the buzz of wasps and possums under the house, far from the bright lights of the city. By this time we had been married for twelve years and had three small children, and here she was, left alone, to manage as best she could, while I flitted off north for my theatrical dalliance. What on earth was I writing this play for anyway, she wondered, when it brought me only empty praise and no paycheck? Generally, she held her tongue, for she was afraid to pit our family well-being against my work. She was married to someone who was . . . well, so single-minded.

In my absence she rambled through the hillsides with the children in our battered red Jeep. Hillary was now old enough to enjoy these randans from an elevated car seat, and they scoured the stream banks and the woods for wildflowers and bugs. To Denise it seemed that Hillary was the most verbal of her three children. Her language began with her interest in the chickadees and merry nuthatches that inhabited the bird feeder outside the picture window, and she squealed "birdy" excitedly every time one came swooping in for a landing. By this time she was beginning to combine words: "We do that," was her enthusiastic response to the suggestion of a little rough-housing.

Her vocabulary was exceptional, partly because she was, like her mother, such a good mimic. She could repeat almost anything you said. On these outings Denise took to enunciating the scientific names of her favorite wildflowers and of her favorite rocks from a college geology course. Sure enough, when she got right up there in Hillary's face and said, "amygdaloidal basalt," Hillary could repeat it, without skipping a syllable.

Fortunately, we had discovered a wonderful caregiver, a tall, cheery, creative country girl named Molly Bell, who was home for the summer from Radford University. Molly's day often began with fixing sandwiches for the picnics by slathering hot-dog mustard on white bread. So, inevitably, she became Molly Mustard, and to this day in our house French's prepared mustard is called Molly

Mustard in her honor. While Molly fixed sandwiches, Hillary rocked incessantly on her rocking horse, and we began to refer to this as the Ride of the Valkyries.

To watch them trundle off down the trail, all in a row toward the stream, was a special treat for me. Like Denise, Molly went off with several books under her arm. Once they found a comfortable rock or log, she would begin the story of the day. There was a ritual. Hillary would pick up a book and hand it to Molly and say plaintively, "Read books." It was a request and a demand and a statement of fact, and Molly would dutifully obey with something like *The Cat in the Hat,* which was one of her favorites, since, coming from a house of felines, this was one cat that did not shed. At the end of the summer Molly presented Hillary with a gift of P. D. Eastman's *Go, Dog. Go!* and signed it "Mawee," the way Hillary pronounced her name.

Beyond the Hume crossroad, we had a strategic friend, a red-haired, high-spirited mineral heiress named Sophie Engelhart who owned a comfortable spread high on Cobbler Mountain and a pack of friendly golden retrievers who dove into her stone-encased pool with abandon, as if they were seals. It also happened that Sophie was friendly with a number of Washington Redskins football players, since she was then dating one of the famous "Hogs," a Yale-educated and very large man named George Starke. So, if you were a young mother, it was fun to hang out there, among those gorgeous hunks, with their perfect bodies. Denise partook of the pleasure often with the children, especially during the blistering days of July.

It was in July of 1983 that Hillary began to exhibit dangerous behavior. At the edge of a steep-stepped Jacuzzi, which Sophie had built next to the pool, Hillary began to take flying leaps into its center, simply expecting someone to catch her before she sank to the bottom or hit her head against the stone. We tried to make light of this bizarre behavior, and gave her the nickname "Fearless Fosdick," but we were disquieted. Then she started to walk straight down the steep stairs of the cabin frontward, having, apparently, no worry whatever about falling. The other two children, even five-year-old Maeve, were still going down those stairs backward.

At about this time we were unnerved by something else: Hillary's acquisition of new words seemed to be slowing down, and this sent Denise scurrying for her Brazelton bible. On this point Dr. T. Berry Brazelton provided her with comfort. As the child focuses on developing gross motor skills, he wrote, the emphasis on language development can slow down. For a time, Denise set this worry aside and enfolded her happy, lively, normal child once again in her arms.

In September it became my turn to manage the household while Denise went off to North Carolina to try a race discrimination case pro bono.

One sunny day when I was alone in the cabin with

her, Hillary got up from the dinner table to go to the kitchen, and suddenly, in a pool of sunlight, she crashed to the wooden floor and lay still on her back, her liquid blue-green eyes staring blankly up at me, fixed, unseeing, vacant. The spell lasted about forty seconds, and then she came out of it, bounced up, and went about her business in the kitchen. I was alarmed. But I had a male response: I ignored the episode—what was I, her mother?—blocked it out, and put it away somewhere, concluding subconsciously that if it did not happen again, it was some fleeting tic that held no significance. I did not mention it to Denise when she returned from North Carolina.

But it did happen again.

Upon her arrival home, Denise got the cold shoulder. This gnawed at her, for Hillary seemed to be saying, as Devin once had before her, with devastating effect, that she was a bad mommy. When bedtime came, Hillary did not look up in her normal fashion and say, "Read books." Instead, she simply handed the books to Denise and turned away.

Before our eyes Hillary was changing. She was withdrawing, and no matter how insistent were our calls to her, she did not seem to heed them. She raced about a hundred miles an hour when she was active, and seemed to have no attention span.

A few days later we noticed that she was walking strangely on her tiptoes. When she ran in the yard, she fell down for no apparent reason. A babysitter reported that she had blithely stepped off a picnic table. More of those terrible staring spells happened. As the symptoms began to pile up, Denise and I decided that we should get her worked up at Children's Hospital in Washington when next we were in town.

But Hillary forced the issue.

The next morning we were again sitting at the picture window, having our breakfast and pointing out the birdies, when Hillary got up and walked again to the kitchen. Once through the door, she turned a few steps to the right out of sight, and then, as if this was an entrance in a horror film, she reappeared in the doorway, shaking violently, crying out, as her eyes rolled up in her head, and she dropped to the floor. There, her body stiffened and she shook grotesquely, her limbs askew and akimbo.

The convulsion lasted about fifty seconds. And then, as if the electrical storm had passed and the sunshine had again popped through, she looked at us wanly, with a touch of confusion and even embarrassment, and smiled angelically.

This was her first undeniable seizure.

CHAPTER THREE

―――――

[1]

A brain seizure, we were to learn soon enough, comes by different names and in different packages. The French have the privilege of the naming: petit mal, grand mal, absence. But none of these names except grand mal, big and very bad, seemed to fit Hillary's first grotesque presentation. In fact, thankfully, she had not had a grand mal seizure, for that can kill you. There was nothing petite about her convulsion, however. An absence seizure seemed to describe those staring spells we'd seen, but that was not quite medically correct. In the end we would know these horrible brain storms by another confusing medical use of the language. Hillary had had her first "partial complex seizure." The convulsion had involved her whole body, brain, and soul in its totality, and the only thing partial about it was that she had survived.

Complex is a different matter. We had no notion about how complicated this was going to be.

Immediately, we got her into the car and rushed her to the little family practice center in Marshall, twelve miles away. From my Chapel Hill experience I was sentimental about medical care outside the big city, especially after Hillary's rough treatment at birth in New York Hospital, but about country medicine in the mountains I was hard-eyed and skeptical. When we had earlier brought Hillary's staring spells and fainting to the attention of this country doctor, his first remark was that "she had just swooned." How quaint, how Southern, how positively Victorian! We knew then he was an idiot.

Now we entered his examining room, and Hillary began racing wildly from one wall to the next, pressing her face against the surface as if she were a cat in a box. Her behavior was erratic, fidgety, uncontrolled. She made no eye contact and seemed only to want to escape from any human that tried to catch her. At last the doctor got it: There was something dreadfully wrong here.

The next stop was the county hospital in Warrenton. It was afternoon by the time we got there, and the other children would soon be arriving home on their buses. And so I left Denise and Hillary in the care of worried hospital specialists and drove home. Once we were collected, the stories of the school day related, the afternoon snacks with Molly Mustard dispensed, the phone rang. Hillary's condition was serious, Denise reported, beyond the ken of the county doctors. They were going by ambulance to Children's Hospital in Washington.

My shock was great. At last there was no more denying the dire situation that Hillary faced. I knew nothing to do but take a long walk. Years later, I would come upon "The Peace of Wild Things," a poem by Wendell Berry, with whom I had come into contact in Kentucky upon occasion, which caught the instinct of that moment:

When . . . I wake in the middle of the night at the least sound
in fear of what my life and my children's lives may be,
I go and lie down where the wood drake
rests in his beauty on the water, and the great heron feeds.
I come into the peace of wild things
who do not tax their lives with forethought
of grief. I come into the presence of still water.

So we set off—Maeve, Devin, our Irish setter, Dara, and I—in search of the place where the blue heron feeds. It was a walk I've never forgotten. We ambled down to the stream and then across the road into a neighbor's fields where I had never taken them before. I did not say much, but there must have been something in my expression that conveyed profound sadness. Maeve was then close to her sixth birthday, and yet she came to me with an understanding that was instinctive and mature, feminine and almost psychic. She took my hand, where on any other walk she would have bounded ahead looking at the wildflowers. Her intuitiveness about emotion has stayed with her into adulthood, but to my knowledge it began there, on that long stroll when she sensed uncertainty where before there was always knowledge, and tragedy where before there was generally happiness. My father had written occasionally about the kindliness of neighbors in mythical Fiery Run, but he had never written about the comfort and succor that children can give along that stream and every other one in the world.

There was to be the kindliness of neighbors that night. As darkness fell, and the children were in bed, and Hillary was somewhere far away in a cold, sterile examining room, being prodded and pricked and regarded quizzically, the word got out. The phone rang around 10 p.m., and it was Sophie Engelhart, inquiring about news I did not have—and about me.

"I just wish I had a good stiff drink in the house," I said offhandedly. About half an hour later I heard a car on the lawn and peered out to see Sophie's truck. When I opened the door, I could see Sophie still in the driver's seat, with the motor still running, as another dear friend, Ann Douglas Atherton, simply handed me a bottle of twelve-year-old bourbon, turned without a word, and climbed back into Sophie's truck.

[2]

Their ambulance ride into Washington had been un-eventful. The two country EMTs kept up a constant chatter about how things were rarely as bad as they seemed, honey, and how the minds of patients in speeding ambulances always ran to the worst scenario. This amiable prattle cut into Denise's anxiety and made the trip more bearable. By the time they were in the emergency room, Hillary had also calmed down considerably. For the skeptical emergency room doctors, she exhibited none of the erratic behavior of a few short hours before.

Denise, however, had a mother's sure instinct that her child was desperately ill. During her electroencephalograph (EEG), the nodes were glued to Hillary's head; it would be days before we could get the goo out and comb her hair properly. The very picture of her child wired up, as the machine beeped and flashed and printed out its spikes and lines, was terrifying enough. When that tiny body was strapped down into a papoose halter and began to slide into the dark cavity for her CAT scan, Denise had the premonition that her child would never be the same. In due course, deep into the evening, after they had been there for several hours, Hillary had a mild seizure, and that was enough to convince the doctor to admit her.

In the morning they were greeted by a young woman who would become a significant presence in our life for the next sixteen years. She was the neurologist, Dr. Joan Conry, a spry woman from Midland, Texas, and pregnant herself. She shared much with Denise—sharp intelligence, a bright disposition, a tart tongue—and yet in that first day she exhibited great sympathy, which was comforting, and great patience, which inspired confidence.

Dr. Conry could feel Denise's raw fear. The first and most profound question was, would Hillary die? Denise had been asking it scores of times in the past twelve hours. No, Dr. Conry did not think so, but on all other matters she was reserving judgment. She posed many questions about whether Hillary had sustained some sort of blow to the head. That she had not made her case curious, but in relating the family history for the tenth time, Denise could only think vaguely of those five days of high temperatures in May. By this time, Hillary's seizures were evident. The tests had located them in the temporal lobe of the brain.

Quietly, Dr. Conry explained the different kinds of brain storms. Hillary's seizures did not quite fit any exact pattern. They were not pure petit mal, but then petit mal could be controlled. The tests showed a slowing of the alpha and beta brain waves. Dr. Conry was inclined to think they were atypical absence seizures. She did not say at first that such seizures are sometimes associated with mental retardation.

Nevertheless, almost intuitively, this label elicited from Denise the second most profound question: Was she ever going to get her daughter back? Hillary's nature was to be cuddly and loving. Yet she had changed before our eyes in the past weeks into something almost unrecognizable.

She was aloof and incommunicative. She was not using her words. Where before we could expect cuddles and kisses and irresistible fireworks, she was now scratching and biting.

Dr. Conry's first response was reassuring. There was no evidence now that Hillary's faculties were impaired. A spinal tap had found no cells in the fluid, the indication of brain infection. It could well be a form of epilepsy, and in modern times, epilepsy was well understood and well controlled in about 75 percent of the cases. The odds were that Hillary Oooi, Oooi, Oh! would return to her normal self in three months. In the interim, until they arrived at a more precise diagnosis, the doctor's description of the condition would be an unspecified encephalitis. It would be some time before we understood that the term *encephalitis* means little more than "brain disease."

Over the coming days, as Hillary's seizures failed to respond to the medication, the discussion between Dr. Conry and Denise at Hillary's bedside ranged over many subjects. Conry's reassurances became more vague as time passed. At one point she said, "I don't know anything about your marriage, but you should know that situations like this put great stress on marriages, and often break them up." When I came to town on one of my visits, she said the same thing a little differently, as if she was intent on signaling heavy weather ahead: "With situations like this, marriages can break up, but they can also get closer."

I stayed in the country with Maeve and Devin during this ordeal, trying to keep things as normal as possible, getting them fed and off to school, and comforted in the evening. Devin was not quite three years old, and so despite knowing that Hillary was sick and away for a few days, he trucked right along. But in her keen intuition about feeling, Maeve, the irrepressible Rainbow O'Leary, who was verging on her sixth year, saw the sadness settling in my face and seemed to appreciate the extent of the crisis. And so we repaired to the typewriter, and with a little technical help from me, she wrote several poems to Hillary.

A LOVE POEM TO HILLARY

BY MAEVE

Hillary, you are a piece of the rainbow
You cheer us up on a rainy day
Your smiles, your words, your games
Are like bright colors on a gray day
When you put your hand to your heart
*   and then out to me,*
It means you love me and I love you.

In these few days, how I've missed
*   Your little kisses*
*   Your head on the table next to mine*
Looking into your blue eyes
*   Forehead to forehead.*
Get well, little Hillary
Get well soon!

OCTOBER 17, 1983

WHEN YOU GET WELL

BY MAEVE

When you get well, Hillary
We will go to the space museum
I will hold your hand
Or would you like me to carry you in?

We will see movies about outer space
    and the planets
And we will look at moon rocks
And see pictures of Saturn,
    the most beautiful planet.

I will show you the inside of a rocket ship
And we will dream about flying to space together.
You and I will plant the American flag
    on the moon . . .
    and a rainbow flag on Saturn.
From Jupiter, we will look down on Hume
And say,
    It's time to go home now.

A day later, it was indeed time to go home. But Hillary was coming home without her seizures under control, without appearing to be any better, with large questions still hanging in the air. She had begun the standard regimen to combat a convulsive disorder. Her main drug was the old standby, phenobarbital, which did not suppress electrical impulses from the epileptic foci, but rather was supposed to block the transmission of the evil electrical impulses to the deeper structures of the brain. In addition, she was prescribed carbamazepine, or Tegretol, as it was better known. This drug was supposed to inhibit the electrical discharges and raise her threshold against convulsion. (*Threshold* was a word that was to take on much greater use in our vocabulary in the time ahead.) And finally, she would take valproate, or valproic acid. This third drug was judged highly effective across the board for minor, major, petit mal, and focal seizures, again by chemically inhibiting the chain reaction that stems from the combustion source and leads to a generalized seizure.

And so we began Hillary's chemical cocktail, or chemical gruel, as I came to call it. But what was the interaction of these drugs when taken together, and in relation to the rest of her body? The literature was ominously candid about this: The interactions of these drugs were not entirely understood.

Still, the plan of action was comprehensive. Dr. Conry was covering the waterfront, and we could only hope that one or all together and in concert would find their way to the sinister source of her storms, tamp it out, and bring back Hillary's sunshine. We would not know about the effectiveness of this regimen for several weeks, since it would take that long for the drugs to reach their therapeutic level.

Denise arrived back at Fiery Run with a very limp child

and an armful of technical medical texts: the *Textbook of Child Neurology, Epilepsy, Taber's Cyclopedic Medical Dictionary,* and so on. She had cut a deal with Dr. Conry: Denise wanted to read whatever Dr. Conry was reading about Hillary's condition, no matter how technical.

At night she plunged into the electricity of the brain: neurotransmitters and receptors, chemicals like dopamine, and my favorite, the synapse. This was the electrical switch between two neurons in a neural pathway where the termination of the axon of one neuron comes into close proximity with the cell body of another. Neuroscientists were interested in the more than 100 trillion of them in the brain, but I was interested in the word itself, which had the sound like the cracking of the whip when lightning strikes your house. Denise tried to sort out sentences like "[Valproic acid] has been found to inhibit the activities of GABA-transferase and succinic semialdehyde dehydrogenase, and in this manner to elevate GABA concentrations within the brain."

At the onset of Hillary's illness we had different ways of coping. Denise's way of wrestling with the monster that had taken up residence in our child's brain was to learn everything she could about it. Subconsciously, the five days in May haunted her, as if she was saying to herself: Never again will something so terrible as this sneak up on me. Knowledge was power. Knowledge was a stout defense. With knowledge, she felt, perhaps she could prevent some further insult from happening.

I had a less-noble attitude. I could not compete with

the doctor's expertise. As a layman, how could I position myself to second-guess the experts? We had to trust them. With the hindsight of twenty-two years, I regard Denise's attitude as the superior one, although there have been a few instances—very few—when my studied distance gave me an appreciation of the larger picture, since I was not caught up in confusing detail. If I think of this shabby instinct as my personal failing, I also think of it as rather typically male. Let her deal with the details. After all, she's Hillary's mother.

In my defense, I only know what was then in my mind. The opening of my play about Jonestown had been scheduled for the following spring, and it would not be long before we went into rehearsal. Adrian was calling about the casting, and I was excited. It had been a long time coming and represented the most artistic enterprise of my literary life to date. I was consumed by it, as much as anything, because it was a collaborative enterprise with wonderful actors and a difficult, brilliant director. It was a break from my solitary work life of the previous thirteen years.

My work was based in emotion, I told myself, and in this case, with the emotion of life, death, and suicide. With the Jonestown story I was navigating in dangerous psychological waters, and I was intensely aware of it. And now I'd been with it for five years.

Throwing myself into the details of Hillary's illness on top of Jonestown was too much. It was more than anybody could bear. Even if so horrible and difficult a subject as Jonestown had not preoccupied me, I had known other writers who stopped writing over events as commonplace as the split-up of their marriage. I had to protect my precious and fragile equilibrium if I was to press on as a writer. I had to be wary of Hillary.

[3]

For the next six weeks we stood by helplessly as we watched Hillary suffer and dwindle. Far from disappearing, her seizures increased in frequency and virulence, to the point where they were coming at the rate of five or six an hour. With firestorms in her brain so frequent and unrelenting, great damage was inevitable. When she was awake and alert, we watched her language disappear, day by day, word by word, until toward December she had only three words: *daddy* (which now to my consternation meant all men), *mommy,* and *birdy*—and then it was only *birdy,* and then nothing . . . nothing but choking, snorting, frustrated guttural sounds as she tried to form old words, but could not find the tools to fashion them.

Only the nipple of her milk bottle seemed to give her any comfort and relief. So we left it in her mouth continuously, knowing full well that it was bad for her teeth to have that sweet, sugary lactose in her mouth all the time. We were beyond worrying about teenage beauty contests now. For the moment, assuaging her suffering was paramount. Minor, momentary relief was all that mattered. Sure enough, by December, she showed signs of tooth decay, and we stopped the practice, but ambivalently.

In early December she was hospitalized again in Washington, but with no real change in her condition or her prognosis. We still rested our hopes in that first grand declaration, that she had epilepsy. In three months she would be back to normal, we told ourselves, even though, in our lucid moments, we were aware that events had passed that declaration by. Hope is important both to patient and doctor, and Dr. Conry was not about to destroy ours.

Several weeks later, in New York, we had our gruesome epiphany. We were there for Christmas, staying in the plush apartment of my old Army buddy Zack Lonstein, who is the funniest man I have ever known, even when he was stealing my girlfriends back in Hawaii in 1967. (Zack, it turned out, passed along his comic streak to his daughter, Shoshanna, who was to have a long and much publicized love affair with the comedian Jerry Seinfeld. Through that patch of Zack's life I had always longed to be at dinner with Seinfeld and the Lonsteins, for I was sure that Seinfeld would be getting the worst of it.) Zack was a pioneer in the computer business and had made a lot of money. Now, with him and his wife, Betty, off in the islands, we had their commodious space on Seventy-ninth Street.

Denise seized the opportunity of being in New York to take Hillary around for a few second opinions. Her first stop was Dr. Esther Silverman. Of that visit we remember nothing; but later, we would have access to Dr. Silverman's records, which had the last visit in May and the December visit on the same page. The May note was unremarkable and upbeat: temperature "resolved" three days earlier, walks alone, knows parts of the face and body, points out objects in picture book. The December note, which described loss of speech, poor eye contact, and jittery, uncoordinated movements, was altogether different. Did Dr. Silverman ever put her May and December notes together and wonder? we asked each other.

Upon the recommendation of our friend Lally Weymouth, Denise also took Hillary to see a well-known neurologist at Columbia Presbyterian Hospital, Dr. Stanley Resor Jr. Ironically, it was this second opinion that cast our fantasies about recovery to the winds. Resor was the son of Stanley Resor Sr., Lyndon Johnson's secretary of the Army, and so he knew Washington, had read a book or two of mine, and knew of our family. After reviewing Hillary's record and examining her closely, he turned to Denise.

"They've told you, I'm sure, that it's not good," he said.

He proceeded to confirm our worst fears. Hillary was going to be retarded. Her language might return—Dr. Resor was not sure—but for that to happen, the seizures had to come under control. Toward that goal, he recommended a drug called nitrazepam, or Mogadon, which was widely used in Iceland for depression caused by the darkness of the endless winter. It was not yet approved in the United States, partly because it was a derivative of the much-abused drug Valium, but we could get it from England, and he would help us.

This sort of catastrophe sometimes happens in accomplished, verbal families, Dr. Resor went on to say. Indeed, something similar had happened to the son of a colleague, who was the chairman of a department at the hospital. But the boy had survived and was now in his twenties.

"What does he do now?" Denise asked.

"On his good days, he can stack boxes in a shoe store," Dr. Resor replied.

There, in that terrible epiphany, the totality of Hillary's life stretched out before us.

And so Denise receded again into her spiritual life. She sought out the Jesuit who had been the spiritual adviser to her family in the Bronx, who had gone on to the distinguished calling as president of Fordham University, and had been friend to mayors and diplomats and presidents. Years before we had asked Father Lawrence McGinley to marry us, as a second choice to Rabbi Sam Schrage. But he, too, had demurred. He was a Jesuit, he explained, trained in an exacting rite. Since I was a Protestant, unwilling to convert, and because we were insisting on designing our own free-flowing, counterculture marriage ceremony in the fashion of the 1960s, he must pass. But Father McGinley had christened Hillary a Catholic at St. Ignatius Church on Park Avenue, after we had agreed to raise her Catholic, and we had stayed in touch.

They met at the Oyster Bar in Grand Central Station. From the moment Denise sat down, she began to talk . . . and talk and talk and talk. Her story and her anguish gushed out of her in a deluge, nattering along so long and so fast that Father McGinley finally threw up his hands to stop her as if she were a breakaway filly. "Whoa, Denise, stop, slow down," he said, and he proceeded to teach her, right there over oyster stew, how to breathe in and out slowly in the Zen manner of transcendental meditation when she got overwrought, uttering slowly, at each down-breath, the word *Jesus*.

[4]

Come what may, we were determined that our Christmas in New York would be a happy one. Denise was home in her favorite city for her favorite day of the year, Christmas Eve. She had lovingly packed up our Christmas orna-ments, each with its special memory and special place in our heart. In the Bronx she went around to her neighbor-hood candy store, where she had lapped up egg creams through her childhood. There she bought a beautiful Bronx Christmas tree from the proprietor, Freddy the Fireman. As they gabbed, she dropped a few lines about our situation.

"Hell, I'll deliver it," Freddy announced heroically, and before long he made the exotic trip down to posh East Seventy-ninth Street, even helping us to put the tree up.

As we began to decorate, Hillary began to have the strongest seizures we had ever seen. For three days they continued unabated, without much letup between them. It was as if the isolated thunderstorms had evolved into a hurricane. When the cyclone finally passed, we surveyed the damage in awe. Hillary looked totally wasted, like a burned-out lightbulb. Deep dark circles sculpted her eyes, and her body was limp and exhausted. She peered helplessly at us with a look of total bewilderment. The satanic force had unleashed its ultimate fury. We took a picture of the ravage, and later, Dr. Conry put it in the front of her medical records, just to remind us what the nadir had been.

Denise struggled to compartmentalize her thoughts and emotions. She wanted to run to someplace safe, but she knew no hospital could help her daughter now. Why did this have to happen at Christmas? In New York? How could she serve up the excitement of the season that Maeve and Devin expected?

The rituals had to go on. We tried to dilute the horror with games and sojourns to the Central Park Zoo, a visit to Santa Claus at Altman's, and, of course, *The Nutcracker.* Leaving Maeve and Devin with their grandmother, we wheeled Hillary to a ceremony of carols at St. Vincent Ferrer Church on Lexington Avenue. As she lay between us in the pew, the choir beautifully sang John Rutter's "Nativity Carol," that lovely, lilting, mournful hymn of Christmas that forever after in our house became known as the "Hillary carol" for the third line of its last stanza:

> *Love in that stable was born,*
> *Into our hearts to flow;*

Innocent dreaming babe,
Make me thy love to know.

On Christmas Eve Granny Eileen came down from the Bronx to cook her signature loin of pork. It was dress-up time, I in my Scottish tartan vest, Denise in her purple Kay Unger cocktail dress. Maeve was dressed in pink taffeta with a cape appointed with gold stars. Tante Maryssa brought a spectacular red rose. By the tree, Devin played with an amazing plastic spaceman that kept popping out its limbs and saying, "Now forming hands and feet." Hillary lay by his side in a daze.

Was this the final fury? What worse could it do now, but kill her? The weak joke became "What happened in Zack's apartment?" as if something naughty had happened there.

But I shudder when I hear it now.

CHAPTER FOUR

---

[1]

Somehow it seemed apt that when I returned from New York to the freezing cabin in the Blue Ridge, ahead of Denise and the children, I found the pipes had burst and the kitchen had been transformed into an ice cavern. I had forgotten to turn the water pump off. The place was a disaster. With ice more than three inches thick on the walls and ceiling, the plumber trudged out from Warrenton through the cold with a huge hot-air blower of the kind that they sometimes used in NFL games in December to keep the players on the bench warm. In horror I watched as the ice cavern was turned into a rain forest.

After the place dried out, some days later, we settled in for the winter of 1984.

It was to be the coldest winter on record in the history of the Republic. For an entire week in January the temperatures hovered around eight degrees below zero. We closed off the drafty living room and huddled together around a wood stove in the dining room, looking wanly at one another. "This, too, will pass" had long since become a family refrain, but for once we were not entirely sure. We were feeling generally snakebit, and this was just another episode of piling on. The electric bill from our baseboard heat that winter soared nearly to the level of our New York rent.

Still, there were magical winter pleasures. The ponds froze, the rocks in the stream stood as solitary mounds in the hard ice, and the snow lay deep on the ground. In this arctic landscape I took our Jeep to one of the long, gentle hills on Fairfield and packed down the snow with the tire treads so that the kids could have an uninterrupted run of nearly a quarter mile, as I waited at the bottom with the hiccup truck and the movie camera. We had some blessings to count. Devin's reading was burgeoning with his Speak & Spell, and Maeve hosted dress-up tea parties with friends from her rural school, little girls with names like Cherish. Still, to Denise it felt as if we were living in the little house on the prairie. Maeve came home from her rural school with stories of her teacher paddling naughty children in front of the class. And a mother of a child in Maeve's class called up one day in excitement, reporting that she'd just "bagged a prize buck" in her driveway. For Denise, the girl from the Bronx, this was a new experience.

My play went into rehearsal in March. The working title at the time was *Kaituma Sunset,* since Jonestown was not far from the muddy, equatorial Kaituma River. On a research trip for the book, I had taken a tramp steamer from Georgetown, Guyana, along the coast and up the river to Port Kaituma, as pink ibises exploded across the bow as if they were warning shots. It was my way of capturing the feel of a real-life *Heart of Darkness.* That trip remains vivid in my mind—partly for the fact that at one point, wearing my sunglasses, I was mistaken for Jim Jones and nearly thrown overboard.

Adrian summoned me for the first ten days of rehearsal to read through the script around the table with the actors. "The table" was Adrian's trademark. In the twenty-five years he had his company in Providence, he had focused more and more on the word as opposed to the decoration of the play. Certainly no slouch for stagecraft, he plied his art to great effect with his resident set designer, the wonderfully incommunicative Eugene Lee. But Adrian's heart lay in the text. That explains why in his later career he staged so much Shakespeare, from Shakespeare in Central Park to the Shakespeare Theatre in Washington.

The weaknesses of the script always emerged in these early sessions. I was fascinated with the contributions that the actors made to changes that were needed. They, after all, were eventually going to stand up there in front of a live audience and speak these lines. I took it somewhat poorly when Adrian was quoted in the *Providence Journal* early on as saying that we had a "barrel load of material," but he wasn't sure we had a play yet. Still, the publicity about the production was copious in Providence and Boston, and lent an atmosphere of real anticipation.

After the first ten days of rehearsal, I was invited to leave. The professionals needed to go to work, undistracted by the presence of the amateur. When I was invited back a few weeks later for the last ten days of rehearsal, I was greeted with substantial restructuring. To these changes I gladly acquiesced, for I knew they had emerged from the hothouse of the rehearsal room. We also changed the title of the play to *Jonestown Express.*

It premiered in mid-May—and flopped. *Time* magazine admired its "bold conception" and provocative ideas and its ability to give those ideas "theatrical life," but generally saw the piece as a mélange of docudrama, sociological argument, fragmented monologues, and musical interludes. Well, yes, I was tempted to reply, Jonestown was like that, but I knew better than to argue with critics. In his *New York Times* review, Mel Gussow was more pointed. He complimented Trinity Rep for giving the play a "vividly theatrical production" and found Richard Kneeland's performance as Jones charismatic and Richard Kavanaugh's portrayal of the camp doctor persuasive. But Gussow bristled with loathing for the evil of Jim Jones— a sentiment, of course, that all Americans, including myself, shared.

But Adrian had worked hard on me to understand and then present the attractive side of Jones at the outset. Jones could not have built two gigantic churches in San Francisco and Los Angeles and a huge following if he had always been a monster. Only if his early allure was on display could the play have movement, even if the movement was toward evil. But Gussow could not swallow Jones's "self justification" and his "invidious comparisons to the martyrs of the past," without the playwright's giving the monster his in-your-face comeuppance right there on the stage.

So I returned to the mountains of Virginia, chastened perhaps, but glad for having had the chance, and satisfied that the piece played to full houses for the remainder of its five-week run. The lead of Gussow's review was "James Reston, Jr.'s knowledge of the nightmare of Jonestown is authoritative." Now I was returning to a nightmare and an evil that was somewhat closer to the bone and the blood.

[2]

During most of 1984 we were focused on the how and the why of Hillary's condition: how to bring her awful seizures somehow under control, and why they were happening in the first place.

Through the first half of the year certain medicines were tried and discarded, while others were kept as their dosages were constantly changed. Phenobarbital had been scrapped early in the year, since it did not appear to have any effect on her electrical storms and made her daredevil behavior worse. High doses of Depakane were tried, but they gave her a permanent trembling and an unsteady gait, so they were discontinued. The sedative Clonopin was prescribed, but it occasioned more rather than fewer absence seizures. Dilantin had its day, but it made her worse and gave her an allergic reaction.

Where was the center? She was becoming a laboratory animal.

In due course her doctors settled upon a triple-headed attack: carbamazepine (Tegretol) for the partial complex seizures, ethosuximide (Zarontin) for the staring spells, and valproic acid for absence seizures. Valproic acid and carbamazepine had been around since the 1960s and had been used effectively and safely in combination. Ethosuximide was somewhat newer, and we were assured that its only known side effect was occasional gastrointestinal upsets in the first few days of its administration. Its use over the next two years in Hillary's case was to become her first contribution to medical wisdom.

If these medicines failed to exert control, we still had options. We could move to steroids or to Dr. Resor's suggestion, Mogadon, from England, and as a last resort, a high-fat diet from hell called the ketogenic diet.

If I had been the Mel Gussow of neurology, I would have given our triple therapy a mixed review. As the drugs reached their therapeutic level, it seemed that Hillary's seizures were lessening. Occasionally, we would be blessed with a patch of up to three weeks when the weather was perfectly calm and sunny. But then the clouds would move in, and storms would break through in a cascading series that went on for several days. Apart from the agony of watching a child suffer, we were frantic at the continuation of the seizures over the months, for only in their control could we rest any hope that Hillary might regain some milestones.

In the late winter she lost another milestone that only the most vigilant doctor would have noticed. She ceased playing peekaboo. Hillary might no longer be able to talk. She did not care so much anymore about books. But when peekaboo went, Denise was devastated, for it had been more than one of her favorite pastimes. It had taken on great symbolic significance about what Hillary could and could not do. It was a precious vestige of that playful theatrical child who could announce herself stage left and give you the Bonaparte salute.

As she receded into her private, unknowable world, we, too, were receding. For the first time in years, we sent out no late Christmas cards. The cards we did get, freighted with the usual good cheer and news of school accomplishments of normal and gifted children, got shoved aside, as if they were some sort of personal rebuke. Our news was never good, and we shrank from telling anyone about our latest disaster.

Though we did not appreciate it, we were working our way through that first phase of self-pity, wondering how Hillary had been singled out for such torture, and why we, good parents and good people and even a little bit religious, had been cursed. In Phase I, you are sure that you are the first and only person on Earth to experience tragedy and loss.

The kindliness of friends in the country was a given. It was a refuge of comfort and joy. There would be many nights when our friends in Warrenton, Harry and Ann Douglas Atherton, and their daughters, Hopie and Lilly, would take Maeve and Devin for the night, so that our elder children could experience a normal evening out and we could concentrate at home on Hillary. It was during this period that Maeve began to take on her role as her mother's comforter and vigilant helper. She was "little Mom." Her mother's bouts of sadness were plain enough to see. To help and to comfort was a blessing, and it also gained Maeve the attention and recognition that she coveted. With their time alone with their mother so short and compressed, Maeve and Devin had to compete for every precious moment.

When we moved to Washington that summer, the coldness and embarrassment of strangers were evident. With Hillary's yips and her strange gait and her impulsive gestures and her hovering parents, it was clear to any passerby that something was wrong with her. Strangers turned away or looked at her curiously as if she were an exotic creature from Mars or the circus. As we met new people, their reaction to Hillary, whether inviting or embarrassed, became a litmus test of whether we chose to pursue the relationship. In our minds we knew this to be unfair, and later we came to realize, in our denseness, that good and well-intentioned people often simply did not know how to react. But we could not help it. It meant that our circle of friends shrank to a precious few.

We were also dense about the toll that the "Hillary test" was taking on Maeve and Devin, for it was also applied to their friends. If Maeve brought home a friend who was inattentive or awkward around Hillary, Denise was apt to point this out to Maeve, and it hurt. It was as if the friend was no longer welcome in our house. This problem lasted into the delicate teenage years. To deal with it, Maeve began to coach her friends about how to act around Hillary beforehand, so they would pass, or at least cheat their way past, the dreaded hurdle. Devin, by contrast, did not suffer as much from this unfair practice. Little boys were not expected to be sensitive. But a little curiosity in Hillary went a long way.

In July 1984 Denise took Hillary to New York again to see yet another world-class expert. She was Dr. Isabelle Rapin, a professor of child neurology at the Albert Einstein College of Medicine in the Bronx with an international reputation for diagnosing the most difficult cases of brain damage. Denise had come upon her book *Children with Brain Dysfunction* and had marked up a number of passages in it that dealt with the loss of language. "When a brain lesion is sustained after language has developed," Rapin had written, "it may affect predominantly the ability to decode language ('receptive aphasia') or to encode language ('expressive aphasia')." This went to our fundamental hope that Hillary would someday recover some language. "In young children recovery from acquired aphasia requiring a shift of cerebral dominance is accomplished at the expense of some cognitive ability. The children regain language, but their intellectual progress rarely returns to its premorbid level." Premorbid level? At this point, we would take any language we could get. We were not sure what "premorbid level" meant to doctors, but we now felt ourselves to be in our postmorbid level.

At Albert Einstein Hospital, about a mile from where Denise had grown up, she found herself in a waiting room packed with mothers from all over the world, from Brazil and Australia and England, and the wait was long. At length, she was ushered into the presence of a genial grandmotherly figure, whose careworn face was in contrast to her flashing, bright eyes. Dr. Rapin apologized for the long wait but said, with a certain fatigue in her voice, that she was brought difficult cases from all over the world, and she felt that she must see them all. For a time she observed Hillary closely while she talked with Denise. Afterward, she drew several conclusions that helped. Hillary could learn, she proclaimed, but her learning would be "visually cued." The damage to her brain, severe as it was, was complete. She did not think further damage would occur.

In her eventual report Dr. Isabelle Rapin salted her conclusions with caveats, but her drift was clear: "It appears, by history at least, that some of the cognitive impairment appears to be reversible when seizures are controlled, although she has never returned to the state she was in prior to the inception of the illness. It is very difficult for me to state whether the marked tremulousness and ataxia (dropping down) are the result of medication, seizures, or the underlying illness."

Here was the nub of the matter. What was the underlying illness? If the seizures were not controlled, how could we hope to reverse her cognitive impairment? Was the medication itself causing her further discomfort and further compromise?

Like the doctors and score of specialists before her, Dr. Rapin could offer no diagnosis. "Mother understands that the prognosis is indefinite but that the probability of complete recovery is not strong," Dr. Rapin concluded. "She clearly knows also that a progressive deterioration has not been ruled out. As is so often the case in such children, time may be the best help in making a diagnosis." This conclusion was cold comfort for us, for time was now the enemy.

Hillary's catastrophic illness had confounded every specialist, no matter what the international reputation. Through 1984 she was given every conceivable test: EEGs, spinal taps, CAT scans, electroretinograms (ERGs), X-rays, more blood sticks than there are fleas in China, and, eventually, a biopsy of her eye. The trouble had been located in the right frontal lobe and in the temporal lobe of her brain. By December 1984, fourteen months after the initial presentation, her brain had shrunk. Ugly, viscous fluid now filled significant spaces where brain matter once had been. The atrophy was palpably visible on the X-rays. Her brain was degenerating.

The frontal lobe is the seat of our emotions, and when it is damaged, as it was in the famous nineteenth-century case of Phineas Gage, when a tamping iron shot through his head, it can lead to erratic and bizarre behavior. (Gage for a brief time became part of P. T. Barnum's freak show, staring out vacantly at the audience as he held the tamping iron that had shattered his skull.) The temporal lobe controls hearing rather than speech and language. Was she deaf? The tests said no. In the language of doctors, her "auditory evoked responses showed normal thresholds."

In all of these consultations with famous and competent doctors up and down the East Coast, the conversation always came back to those five days of high temperatures in May 1983. But still the experts were confounded, for the natural defenses of the body (especially the brain) against invasion from sinister forces are incredibly strong. In the architecture of the human body, we had been told, one of God's brilliant touches was the "blood-brain barrier," which prevented infections from the lower forty from moving upward into the brain. How could that evil seed have blown past that Chinese wall? Or what was even more horrible to contemplate: What if it was on the inside all the time, a mole and traitor to its own warm body? To use the hateful computer language, what if this disease had been preprogrammed in her genes? What if we had placed the traitor there ourselves, mixed in the very juices and fluids of our prodigious love?

Still, a stark fact remained about those five days in May. In pronouncing the infection to be viral, the doctors had not ordered hospitalization and had not demanded a spinal tap. This tap might have shown cells in the spinal fluid, and with that, aggressive treatment might have, at the very least, limited the scope of the disaster. It was not inconceivable that those five days of untreated fevers had, in and of themselves, triggered an underlying illness that might otherwise have remained dormant.

[3]

"If you hear hoofbeats, think horses, not zebras," goes the old medical saw, but toward the end of 1984 the doctors had looked at all the obvious ailments for Hillary. Now they began to look into esoteric diseases. We entered into this zebra hunt with some trepidation. Dr. Conry had said, "All the labels they will look at now are worse than what we have been considering so far."

In all our interviews over the previous fourteen months, the doctors had been interested in our ancestry and family history. To me these questions had the aura of a medieval examination. Denise and I were a boring mix of Irish and Scottish blood, and the reports all took note, as they did in the days of Eleanor of Aquitaine, that there was no consanguinity between Denise and me (unless it had been in Viking days). As a child I had been severely dyslexic. While this interested the doctors, I was disappointed that they seemed disinterested in my bus accident at age seven. Cracked brains from bus accidents evidently do not get passed along from one generation to the next. I had confessed to having two second cousins who were mentally retarded. Denise had a great-aunt with "spells," but what that meant at the turn of the century was anybody's guess.

In December 1984 the gumshoes from the genetics department at the National Institutes of Health entered the case. The overriding question was whether Hillary was still suffering from a degenerative disease that was genetically determined. Dr. Conry did not think so, but in the absence of a firm diagnosis, she expressed the customary caution. We were all operating on the assumption that the satanic seed had entered Hillary's brain in those five days in May, had done its worst, and then died in its own carnage. Still, when the NIH genetics report came in, it honed in on the area of degenerative disease in the gray matter of the brain.

We were now into those dire speculations that Dr. Conry had warned us about. The labels all seemed to have grotesque names attached to them: Gaucher's disease, Niemann-Pick disease, Fabry's disease, Leigh's disease, Alpers' disease, Menkes kinky hair syndrome, Tay-Sachs disease. We could not help wonder if we were on the trail of a rarity that would someday be called Hillary Reston disease. These named diseases were all chemical imbalances in the metabolism of the brain, the so-called storage and nonstorage disorders. With many of them life expectancy was short, and death was gruesome.

On the strength of tests and logic and her clinical history, the NIH report ruled out the named labels one by one, including the possibility of an inherited storage or nonstorage disorder or of a metabolic disorder—all, that is, except one, a label that formed in the mouth like a sour prune: ceroid lipofuscinosis. With this monstrous disease, death occurs toward the fifth year, preceded by blindness and then dementia. "If this tragic child has a diagnosable disorder," the NIH geneticist concluded, "ceroid lipofuscinosis would be the entity that would be most consistent with her clinical course." If she has a diagnosable disorder . . . the phrase rang in our ears.

Ceroid lipofuscinosis involves the excessive storage of fatty pigments in the smooth muscle cells. This overabundance damages the nervous tissue and accounts for walking problems and dropping down. Gradual blindness comes later, before the person goes crazy and then dies. Dr. Conry was skeptical. And she was also far too politically correct to say that lipofuscinosis also goes by the name of amaurotic familial idiocy. Familial idiocy? Surely not in the brilliant Reston and Leary families. It is a disease inherited in the so-called autosomal recessive pattern. That meant, at least from the standpoint of logic, that for Hillary to have gotten the disease, both Denise and I had to be carriers of this abnormal gene.

So we had done this to our own child. It also meant

that our elder children, normal and even gifted in every respect, had a 67 percent chance of being carriers.

Three tests existed to confirm or deny the speculation: a conjunctival biopsy (i.e., taking a sample from the white part of her eyeball, for that was where the excessive storage could most easily be determined); a skin biopsy (i.e., taking a plug from her arm); and finally, the easy part, a twenty-four-hour urine collection. And so, in early December 1984, we packed Hillary up yet another time and took her to be pricked and poked and wrung out like a dishrag.

On January 15, 1985, I came home early in the evening to find Denise already in her nightgown and robe. She called me somberly into the study, sat me down, and told me that Dr. Conry had called. The result from the conjunctival biopsy was in. It was positive. Hillary had the disease. Dr. Conry had conveyed the news flatly, as if she was stunned and disbelieving. She had used the word *appears*—the test "appears" to be positive. She would order further tests. And she rang off.

So Hillary had it. Soon enough, she would start to lose her eyesight. And then? We decided not to tell the children and fell into each other's arms.

CHAPTER FIVE

Occasionally, after I put her to sleep, I would tarry by Hillary's bedside and wonder what she was thinking. What did she feel about all this? What were her dreams? and her hopes? What visual images did she have in her mind, and what could she remember? I wondered how she could bear all this pain and what it felt like when she had a seizure. After one of her storms, we might think she looked scared, but was it really fear or something else? I did not know. At other times, after a storm abated, her face would break into the most beatific smile and she would chirp happily. It was at these moments that she looked her most angelic. Was this relief? or some surge of pleasure after pain? Was she in fact an angel? How far we have come, the historian in me would say, from the days of Salem, when epileptics were regarded not as angels but as witches.

How much, in her fragile innocence, did she understand? Or was she in some unfathomable state of perpetual confusion and bewilderment? The doctors always seemed to look at her as an ill child, as a vessel of a puzzling chemical imbalance or shorted electrical circuitry somewhere in the sloppy wiring of her 100 trillion synapses. Only we, in our own fragile innocence, seemed concerned with her as a whole person in all the glory of her humanness. As her problems had grown more complex, we found ourselves more and more in the hands of specialists. The impenetrable medical jargon baffled me. I was developing a refrain: "Who is looking over the whole person?"

I liked to think that internally she was still developing normally. It was just that she couldn't express it to the outside world, for it had not been her language center in her left hemisphere, but her memory center in the right hemisphere, that had been assaulted. And anyway, Dr. Conry had told me that the brain in a child under two years was very plastic and had great ability to adapt to insult. Dr. Conry persisted in her view that it was the seizures themselves that were blocking Hillary's speech. There was even a technical name for this condition: Landau's aphasia.

And so I fantasized. If she had several hundred words before the five days of horror in May 1983, perhaps she was still building her secret internal vocabulary at a fast clip, just like her peers. The worst part, I thought, must be her frustration at not being able to communicate all she was experiencing. Once as gregarious as Denise, now she had been forced to be internal like me. Well, that was all right. One could learn to live within oneself. Regularly, I had the recurring dream of the moment she began to speak again.

Denise was also dreaming. As usual, the mother's dreams were more vivid. Noticing that in recent times Hillary had been watching her mouth as she spoke, Denise interpreted this as the precursor to speech. And so, in her mother's dreams, Hillary began to speak in exactly the same baby voice she had used before she became sick. There was no disconnection, no interruption. Everything was again the way it had been. When Denise awoke to find that it was not so, she was devastated and would dissolve into tears. After a long series of these unrequited dreams, they turned to nightmares. Often I would have to roust her out of her sleep, when she cried out in the night, imagining in her nightmare that dogs were coming to devour Hillary or that her child had been left inadvertently on top of the car or had been kidnapped. Once as Hillary was swaddled for a CAT scan and then slowly eased into the machine's belly, Denise had a vivid fantasy of her child being rolled into a mechanical grave.

The children were also having their own fantasies. When Maeve, the intrepid little mom, held Hillary in her arms during a seizure, she imagined her sister to be drowning in a pit of snakes. Like me, Maeve often got up in the night to visit Hillary's bedside, just to make sure that she was alive and breathing. Occasionally, she would poke Hillary in the ribs just to get a response. Devin's fantasies were more meteorological and nautical. In his imagination a seizure launched his sister onto a vast stormy ocean during a typhoon. This gave a whole new spin to the term *brain storm.*

Meanwhile, I seemed to have an infinite capacity for deluding myself. Only a few days before the diagnosis of ceroid lipofuscinosis, I wrote a cheery note to Dr. Conry about how well Hillary seemed to be doing after the crisis in New York and after we stopped the ghoulish ketogenic diet: "I feel that since Hillary has come off the ketogenic diet, she has been worlds better. Her face no longer has that sick, haunted, tormented look. She is happy and active. She talks more, with a few recognizable words, used appropriately. She concentrates better on activities. The old Hillary is back, and I feel under the circumstances she has a much better chance to learn and develop." To say the least, that was a lapse into temporary euphoria.

Once a little friend of Maeve's came over and looked down on Hillary's wasted body as she lay on the couch, languidly putting one LEGO on top of another and occasionally shooting a wary glance at a stranger. The friend said unforgettably, "It must be hard to be Hillary."

Yes, I thought, it must be hard to be Hillary. It takes a seven-year-old to remind us of it.

We began to sense in Hillary something that was beyond language. It was beyond her suffering, her bewilderment, her frustration, beyond her Millsian pleasures and pains, beyond her endless visits to doctors' offices and hospital laboratories. It was an internal strength. She had (mostly) wonderful medical care, but her doctors alone could not pull her through, especially not if she really had this daunting, rare disease. Nor could we do it. She had to do it herself. We knew that she was becoming inured to the constant pricking and poking. Her pain threshold was becoming very high. But it was beyond that. She was tough, mentally and spiritually. It finally dawned on us. She had a ferocious will to live.

We began to call her the Unsinkable Molly Brown.

Through the spring of 1985 the publication of my Sherman book, first in *The New Yorker,* and then in book form, bought me some relief from the relentlessness of Hillary's situation. For Denise and Hillary, there was no letup. Denise was at the height of her mother's anxiety, calling Dr. Conry almost every day with questions. Needless to say, Hillary was not the doctor's only patient, and Dr. Conry quickly tired of this. Instead, she proposed a weekly face-to-face meeting. For me the frequent contact had the bitter taste of a death watch. Our doctor seemed to be preparing us for an inevitable decline straight ahead, and, until the other tests proved otherwise, the doctor continued to subscribe to the likelihood of the ceroid diagnosis. In fact, Dr. Conry's impulse for the meetings was different. If patients are calling you daily, she felt, you are not meeting their needs.

The other tests, especially the urinalysis, were maddeningly slow in getting processed. Two months after their administration, the results were "still pending." Such tests took a long time to analyze, we were told when we complained, and the waiting line was long. For a laboratory technician viewing a forest of plastic specimen cups, we were just another cup and another set of figures. At least, that was how we imagined it, and accepted meekly the standard explanation. Only many months later—in fact, well into the summer—months in which we tried to come to terms with the death sentence that one laboratory test had handed down on our daughter, did we get another explanation. Hillary's urine samples had been placed in a refrigerator at NIH behind some other containers and had been forgotten. It was a clear case of negligence that cost us six months of unneeded anxiety.

If through this period I had hovered quizzically over Hillary, wondering about the mystery of her, Denise's stance was more elemental. Since her attention to Hillary had been constant, Dr. Conry had asked her to keep a chart of Hillary's activity. It read like the weather report: flurries of mild seizures, strong seizure at school, bad cold, good day. For six months Denise had tried to shield her other two children, telling little lies to Maeve and Devin when they looked up at her in anguish and asked if Hillary was going to die. The strain was evident; the toll on the family was great. Now, in her private moments, Denise would enfold her third child in her arms, smother her with kisses, and cry out, in supplication, but also in anger, "Don't leave me. Don't leave me," as if to impart her street-fighter strength to her child. They were both fighters.

And Denise was angry. She was angriest of all at her God, this cruel *pater noster,* who was allowing this innocent creature to suffer and perhaps to die. She was angry in her certitude that we were good people who did not deserve this. Between her Catholicism and her feminism, a fault yawned open. The heavy-handed male image of the Old Testament Jehovah had never been her cup of tea. As he had deserted her, she deserted him now. She turned, instead, in her prayers, to the nurturing image of the Virgin Mary, the *madonna dolorosa,* the Queen of Angels, the mother who had lost a son. Throughout her childhood Denise had been to countless novenas with her mother, and now words of the Memorare rolled out with new meaning.

> *Never was it known that anyone that fled*
> *   to thy Protection,*
> *implored thy help, or sought thy intercession*
> *   was left unaided.*
>
> *Inspired by this I fly up to Thee, O Virgin of*
> *   virgins, my mother.*
> *To Thee I come; before Thee I stand, sinful and*
> *   sorrowful.*
> *Oh, Mother of the Word Incarnate, despise not*
> *   my petition,*
> *but in thy mercy hear me and answer me.*
>
> *Amen.*

I met Denise's profound sorrow and fury with less-strong, Protestant fatalism and male denial. If the horrid ceroid lipofuscinosis diagnosis was confirmed scientifically, beyond any doubt, I would try to deal with it then. For now, I turned speculation aside. Hillary's palpable suffering, rather than her eventual prognosis, concerned me most. To the extent that I thought about Divine awareness or intervention at all, my mind would drift back to Reverend Bill Coffin's sermon after the death of his son: "God is dead set against all unnatural deaths. . . . when the waves closed over the sinking car, God's heart was the first of all our hearts to break." Maybe. Perhaps. But what about a child's unnatural suffering? I wanted to ask. Coffin had also scoffed at the notion of God as the Cosmic Sadist. Where was God's heart now as he witnessed the seemingly endless persecution of this child?

Through the spring, we watched anxiously for the first signs of Hillary going blind. Dr. Conry had made it clear: If she had a degenerative disease, she would unmistakably start to go downhill. Instead, we noticed something quite different. Her seizures were fewer. She was not falling down as much. She was starting to "vocalize," a new word we had acquired for Hillary's heavenly babble. "Dee-dee-dee" had become a very sweet sound indeed.

Moreover, it had long tormented us that when she was sitting on the floor, she took an inordinate interest in tiny flecks of dirt. I tried to break her of the disgusting habit by calling her a nitpicker. It was as if, by making fun of this practice to someone who had no "receptive speech," I might get her to stop it. Such was the game I was playing with myself. Now, suddenly, her attention to tiny objects was significant. One day in the late spring when I caught her picking staples out of the rug in my study, I swept her up in my arms and gave her a huge hug. We had the distinct feeling that Hillary was getting marginally better rather than declining.

Meanwhile, Dr. Conry scoured the country for a specialist on ceroid disease. This search turned up Dr. Paul Dyken in Mobile, Alabama, the chairman of the neurology department at the University of South Alabama. Not only did Dyken know more about the disease than anyone else in the world, he had first coined its label in 1967. How rare was the disease? Dr. Dyken had seen fewer than two hundred cases of it in his entire career. He was now experimenting with a new protocol that had not cured but at least had retarded the progression of the disease in some patients. Dr. Dyken's protocol was a cocktail of antioxidants, including vitamins E and C and selenium. In Dr. Conry's opinion, these agents were benign. It could not hurt Hillary to take them. So she joined Dr. Dyken's exclusive club in February 1985.

In July Denise took Hillary to Mobile. For that mossy trip she had the company of one of her oldest friends and colleagues, Pam Horowitz. Pam and Denise shared the privilege of serving the great Chuck Morgan in the heady battles for civil rights and the Nixon impeachment at the American Civil Liberties Union, and later came together in Chuck's private law firm. This wonderful friend had been a rock of support and good cheer as we raised our children. Since she had once lived in Mobile and had many friends there, Pam proposed to make this a girls' outing to the beach, full of po' boys and long soaks and frolics on the white sand of Destin, Florida. It's hard to overstate how important a friend's arm and shoulder and laughter can be in an anxious moment. I was no help. I was in Japan on assignment for *Esquire* and *The New York Times Magazine.*

In his Mobile office, Dr. Dyken had reviewed the ocular workup that reported, in the dry language of science, "abnormal intracellular inclusions suggestive of ceroid lipofuscinosis." With annoyance he noted that the results of the skin biopsy and urine collection were still pending six months later. The plan that day had been to administer an MRI, a test using the magnetic resonance imaging device that was then in its early stage of deployment. For the test the patient needed to be asleep, and so Hillary was given a powerful sedative. Five hours later, she was still running around a mile a minute. It was getting toward 5 p.m. and the nurses wanted to go home.

But when he turned to the patient herself, and looked deeply into her lovely blue-gray eyes, Dr. Dyken doubted immediately that she had the disease.

"If she has it, I can't confirm it," he said clinically. If there was evidence, it would turn up first in the eyes. Six months after the diagnosis, Hillary showed no signs of the telltale discoloration in her eye pigment.

Could it be that the data from the January eye biopsy

had been misread? Was it possible that the scientists had erred?

Hillary, Denise, and Pam drove off in high spirits. An hour later in a restaurant in Pensacola, Hillary at last fell fast asleep.

In fact, the possibility of a mistaken analysis of the data had long been in Dr. Conry's mind. At Denise's urging, she had looked into the possibility of a "false positive." With an abundance of caution, she had sent the data to a world-class specialist in Montreal, Canada, for a second opinion. At about the same time the girls were driving to Pensacola, Florida, Dr. Stirling Carpenter was writing this letter in Montreal:

"Reviewing the electron micrographs from this patient's conjunctival biopsy, I do not see anything to make me think of storage disease. There are lysosomes in some cells, but these look to me like normal lysosomes. Note that their surrounding membrane is quite distinct, and that a little pale band usually separates it from the dense contents. That is not a feature in storage disease. These lysosomes are also pretty small."

And when Denise and Hillary were flying home, unaware of this astonishing turnabout, some genius at NIH finally discovered Hillary's urine cups in the refrigerator, ran his test in a few minutes, and found none of the telltale dolichols to suggest a storage problem in the nervous system.

Hillary had her reprieve.

CHAPTER SIX

[1]

During the first eight months of 1985, in the throes of this family crisis, I was fortunate in my professional diversions. Past work was coming to fruition, and new work propelled me forward. I found that I had nearly mastered the art of divorcing my literary pursuits from my personal sadness. In January of that year, *The New Yorker* finally published my lengthy article on General William Tecumseh Sherman's march across the South in the Civil War. Under the gentle sensibility of the esteemed editor, William Shawn, the narrative had been detoothed. I was disappointed that the article lacked the embroidery of a classic *New Yorker* sketch of the famous Augustus

Saint-Gaudens statue of Sherman in front of the Plaza Hotel. But I could scarcely complain. Two months later, the book version, *Sherman's March and Vietnam,* was published. In it the narrative reclaimed its teeth. In the book I projected from my Sherman tracing and made connections, in a series of essays, between Sherman's ethics and the prosecution of the Vietnam War. The last of the essays dealt with the demise of the only GI buddy of mine whose name is etched in the Vietnam Memorial in Washington. He was Ron Ray, with whom I had trained in intelligence work at Fort Holabird in Baltimore, and who had been killed in 1968, pointlessly, in Hue during the Tet offensive. Ron had volunteered for Vietnam after a spat with a colonel about playing on his unit's softball team, and never fired a weapon in anger. This pointless death has always been my symbol for the war's futility and waste of a generation.

In general, the fate of a book takes several months to unfold. For once, I was happy with the protracted process. Through the spring months, as Hillary's fate with ceroid lipid disease hung in the balance, I relished the Sunday ritual of watching the reviews roll in. To my pleasure, they were uniformly favorable. It amused me to see that the graphics that often accompanied these considerations featured General Sherman's grizzled visage set against a backdrop of jungle vegetation and Huey helicopters.

Meanwhile, *Esquire* and *The New York Times Magazine* asked me to go to Japan for separate magazine assignments. In the early summer, as Denise prepared to take

Hillary to Alabama, I flew off, first class, to Tokyo. The *Times Magazine* assignment had a worthy theme: to delve into the way Japan taught World War II history to its children. It was a theme that had long fascinated me from my work on Vietnam and the uneven American way of coming to terms with that despicable war: How did any country, Germany, Japan, or the United States, ever teach the dark chapters of its recent history to its children? I was excited about my visit to Hiroshima, where I'd been asked to teach a class on war guilt and responsibility at Hiroshima University.

At the top of my private agenda was to meet the Japanese novelist (and subsequent winner of the Nobel Prize for Literature) Kenzaburō Ōe. Ōe had written extensively about Hiroshima. Beyond his literary efforts, he was the uncompromising leader in the Japanese antinuclear movement and a strong voice for the view that Japan, as the only victim of nuclear warfare, must remain a model for disarmament to the world. Ostensibly, there was good reason for me to contact him for the *Times* piece.

But my real motive was to talk with him about his novel *A Personal Matter.* It was a book I greatly admired and that bound Ōe and myself metaphysically with a strange but strong tie. There were differences in our situations, of course. The abnormality of his child had presented itself at birth. Hillary had been a rich, vibrant, wonderfully complex personality nearly two years old when she had been struck down with all the randomness of a lightning bolt.

Ōe was not an easy catch. Notorious for the resolute protection of his privacy, he did not immediately respond to my overtures. For many months he had granted no interviews. It was said that he was working on a group of essays about America, and he did not wish to be disturbed. But I persisted, and Ōe must have sensed a special urgency beyond my announced purpose to discuss with him the dark recesses of Japan's modern psychology.

He met me at the train station not far from his home in the pleasant Seijo section of Tokyo. There, in the midst of the fluid throng, I did not recognize him immediately. In my mind was a twenty-year-old photograph from the jacket of *A Personal Matter.* It showed a vigorous, broad-shouldered, bespectacled, intellectual figure with prominent ears and a remote, independent air, riding a bicycle with his young son. On the book jacket, the boy looked perhaps four years old, and he had the same prominent ears as his father. In the photograph the child looked perfectly normal. Before me now stood an older, diminutive man with a shy and deferential manner. We bowed to each other decorously.

For all his vaunted elusiveness, Ōe could not have been more gracious as we walked through the narrow streets of Seijo, past the walled mansion of the actor Toshiro Mifune. We shared a common political outlook. But these opinions were not the core of the matter. Rather, the situation of his son, struck down at birth with a congenital abnormality of the skull, furnished my urgency. I wanted to tell him about Hillary. I, too, had a picture of myself riding a bicycle with Hillary on the backseat.

In literary gossip, the affliction of Ōe's son was often mentioned as a turning point that had a profound influence on his later work. It was said that after his personal tragedy he had become brusque and distant to the point of paranoia in his personal relations, as he became more passionate in his social and political beliefs about the aftereffects of Hiroshima.

In the past three years, I had begun to wonder if my own personality and later work would be similarly affected. I sensed in myself not an intensification of my social passions but a diminishing of them. I was turning inward, becoming more quirky, distant, even paranoid. I was operating constantly on the extremes of joy and depression. I lived in constant dread of Hillary's next setback.

In three hours of animated conversation, we touched upon our bond only once, fleetingly. There was not much to say. I told him how I identified with the book's rage and the desire for release in outrageous, depraved behavior from the horror of a dying child. I admired his searing honesty. I had been moved, I told him, by the affirmation of life that emerges from despair at the end of the novel.

I had been particularly taken by his image of a mine shaft, narrow and deep. "But what I'm experiencing personally now," says Ōe's character, Bird, "is like digging a vertical mine shaft in isolation; it goes straight down to a hopeless depth and never opens on anybody else's world.

So it won't result in so much as a fragment of significance for anybody else. Hole-digging is all I'm doing, futile, shameful hole-digging; [I'm] at the bottom of a desperately deep mine shaft and I wouldn't be surprised if [I] went mad!"

For the six months we waited for Hillary to go blind and then crazy before she died, I, too, resided in that mine shaft, a hole without light, without a side tunnel, with no apparent escape hatch. It was a personal matter, narrow and deep, and had no relevance to anyone else's world. If I were French, I suppose this would be called ennui. If I were Sartre, it would be *La Nausée*.

There was no way to make grief horizontal. It could not be spread sideways. It was not like Tom Sawyer's cave, where a side passageway might bring the hope of escape, for all the side passages so far had been blind alleys. In that mine shaft my head swam with dizziness. I tried not to look down—but then, to look up seemed pointless. So, afraid to look up or down, I stared straight ahead into the blank wall, blankly.

As the modern world turns, I was told I was depressed, and should go for psychiatric counseling. Perish the thought. I dismissed it out of hand. My inner life, so central to my work, could not be touched. It would be a violation. To enter counseling was to end my career as a writer. That was how I felt, for I had seen it happen to others. To "talk a story out" was never to get it down on paper.

Inevitably, one presents a mask to the world. You are

told that things are going to be all right, and how well you are handling "this thing." What else can others say? What can they really do? It is a dangerous time for friends, for they must be aware of the shame and the embarrassment and rage that comes with a man's acute distress. With a kind of perverse pleasure, I watched their awkward shifting about as, fearful of touching the nuclear button, they searched for the right thing to say.

When friends said I was handling this well, that everything was going to turn out all right, I wanted only to shrink away. I seethed with the outrageous anger I had found in Ōe's book, wanting to cry out, No, you don't understand, it is not going to be all right; and no, I am not handling this well. I longed for release from this suffocating situation. I wished I could escape in exotic, private dissipation. I envied Ōe's character, Bird.

Men are not well suited to emergencies with children. "The feeling had been growing in him slowly since he had learned that his baby was a freak," Bird says in Ōe's novel. "Now he wanted to drop out of this world for a while, as a man drops out of a poker game when he had a bad run of cards." Like most men, my impulse was to block, to deny, to leave it to the women. We become shut out, but the truth is, we want it that way. The brave stiff upper lip is expected—it is the manly thing to do—although an occasional relapse into public tears is allowed for the New Age guy. We cannot admit that this avoidance is not manliness, but cowardice.

And yet, when I returned from Japan and learned

from Denise that Hillary did not have that rare scourge of waxy pigments in her tissues, I discovered that there is a corollary to Ōe's mine shaft. Joy, too, is vertical. It is a veritable laser beam of joy that has no terminus. It is mine alone, totally a personal matter. It cannot be shared. As Hillary had her reprieve and then subsequent reverses, I seemed alternately to live in the stratosphere and in the lithosphere.

My relations with those who have experienced something like "this thing" have been the easiest. As with Ōe, the shared adversity is usually unspoken. It is realized in a giving that takes another form and shape. To Ōe I was a perfect stranger, and yet he opened up, uncharacteristically. He grappled with cerebral issues about modern Japan until I ran out of questions. It was a favor. Lawyers might call it professional courtesy. It was human courtesy.

As time passed I remembered less what I subsequently wrote about Japanese education than what Ōe had written about grappling with the fate that was handed to him (and me), and then his affirmation of life with action.

"It's so I can stop being a man who's always running away," says Bird at the end of the story. "All I want is to stop being a man who continually runs away from responsibility."

[2]

From the ravages of ceroid lipofuscinosis, with its promise of blindness, dementia, and death in the first decade of life, Hillary had had her reprieve all right, but that did not alter her basic situation or ours. We were back into the ether of the unknown. Dr. Conry tried to put a positive spin on our groping. All the specific diseases that might still be left for Hillary were even worse than ceroid disease, she said. What's in a label anyway? Only later did we learn that even ceroid lipofuscinosis applied to a family of syndromes, not a single, specific disease.

Nor did our gnawing uncertainty alter our day-to-day patterns. We were contending with a child that could neither feed nor dress herself, who was climbing dangerously on furniture and cabinets with no sense of caution, and whose brain seizures were still only partially controlled.

In mid-1985, a year and a half after the onset of the disease, we finally found a drug that provided at least some measure of control. It was the drug first recommended to us two years earlier by Dr. Stanley Resor Jr., known by its British name of Mogadon (nitrazepam). And British it was. For Mogadon was still in clinical trials in the United States, and could not be dispensed in American pharmacies. It was, however, widely available in Europe, especially in Iceland of all places, where it was frequently used by psychiatrists in hypnosis, since the pill is a variant of Valium. And so we began a ten-year association with a quaint, old-fashioned apothecary in London, D. R. Harris & Co. Ltd., Chemists and Perfumers, on St. James's Street.

With Mogadon, Hillary's seizures dwindled from daily to occasional. Our dreams of her beginning to talk seeped through again. We were warned that Mogadon sometimes has a "honeymoon" effect, that it can lose its effectiveness after only a few months. But Hillary still takes it twenty years later. Some honeymoon! We came to view it as a godsend.

Our English apothecary, it turned out, was quite a famous shop in London. Founded in 1790, it had established a reputation during the Industrial Revolution for its lavender water, its classic cologne, and its English flower perfumes, which it dispensed to ambassadors, field marshals, and admirals at the nearby Court of St. James, as well as to the fastidious rakes and dandies who hovered around the exclusive gentlemen's clubs on St. James's Square. In 1938 the shop had received the Royal Warrant as the chemist to Her Majesty, the Queen Mother.

Once we were reassured that we were doing nothing illegal by getting this medicine from abroad, we were regularly in touch by telephone and fax with this venerable institution. The prescription for Mogadon would be sent, and a few weeks later a little box, perfectly packaged in brown wrapping paper, would arrive, with all the appropriate customs markings, as well as the seal of the Queen Mum all the way from London's clubland.

From time to time, Denise became anxious when the box was a few days late, for we were always terrified about running out. She would call London secretly, only to hear the soothing bright voice of the clerk at D. R. Harris say that yes, indeed, the medicine had gone out in the same day's post and should be arriving promptly.

A few years into this association, Denise paid a personal

visit to D. R. Harris. The shop was, as she imagined, entirely wood-paneled, with perfect little wood-trimmed glass display cases with such special items as boar's hair shaving brushes and ivory-handled toothbrushes. At last, Denise could put that bright English voice together with a fresh-faced clerk named Eliza, who immediately called down to the head chemist. In a few moments Mr. Trevor Harris, M.P.S., the managing director himself, appeared in his white coat, wiping his hands on an embroidered hand towel, to greet Denise warmly as a very important client. She in turn thanked him profusely for the medicine that over the years had been so important to her daughter.

Afterward, Denise, reveling in this royal moment, went around the corner to Turnbull & Asser, where she bought me a garish blue shirt with a removable white collar, an item I could not put on until I was fifty years old and becoming eccentric.

[3]

As Hillary approached her fourth year, we entered the realm of the handicapped child. I moved into this circus world with trepidation. I could look with love and longing and wonder at my own child and never think of her as particularly different—special perhaps, but not different. She was merely mine. But when I saw her in school, in the company of misshapen children, some of them far worse off than she, and who had none of her physical beauty or her genuine cuddly charm, who indeed were difficult to look at in their deformities and their ill-fitting, hand-me-down clothes, I shrank away again as quickly as possible to crawl down my dark and narrow pit. It was only in the company of others "like her" that we understood the full impact of her losses.

In Hillary's formal education, we were thrown into the superb, caring community of teachers in special education. If there is a group of professionals anywhere with bigger hearts and greater dedication, I can't think who they might be. In this magical oasis, so totally opposite from the indifference and downright scorn for Hillary that we encountered in the general population, we were among people who cherished and valued their poignant wards. They saw their students as people who were not defined by their handicaps but simply had intriguing difficulties that needed to be worked through. They stood aside and viewed Hillary quizzically, racking their brains about creative things to try. And they engaged us in a constant dialogue about new things to do. The challenges they faced excited them, and small triumphs—like the building of a three-block tower, for example—exhilarated them. We were exhilarated in turn. Over the years many of these heroes would nurture and educate Hillary. Not infrequently they bore the scars of their commitment in the form of scratches and bruises. Occasionally, to our profound distress, we would get a note from school asking us, almost apologetically, to cut Hillary's fingernails.

In her preschooling Hillary was educated at a facility called Montgomery Primary Achievement Center (MPAC), an institution run by the Montgomery County Association for Retarded Citizens. There she fell under the aura of her first mentor, a soft-spoken, gentle woman with a keen sense of humor and great wisdom named Jean Witt. Most of Jean's students in those days were boys, since the laser beam of retardation tends to singe more boys than girls. For so adorable a little lady like Hillary to enter her classroom was a special treat.

Instead of seeing her as an object, Jean viewed Hillary as an intriguing challenge, and she set out to socialize her. Jean was the first of Hillary's teachers (but scarcely the last) to appreciate the native intelligence that lay smothered beneath her global impairments. More than smart, Hillary was also wily and manipulative, and this bemused us all, for femininity was on display in its pristine essence. Because she was cute and lively, she quickly became the darling of the school. Perhaps she would have her day as a beauty queen after all.

At this point Hillary was a bundle of frayed wires and loose ends. Music hurt her tender ears, and water overstimulated her nerves. Any sort of pressure or vibration made her recoil. Her high-wire acts on windowsills and cabinet tops were at their zenith, and she was regularly busting out windows with coffee cups. She continued to drop down unexpectedly from her ataxia, but she could also drop down deliberately, testing Denise's physical limits to lift her. In public we found ourselves constantly apologizing to those around us, whether in a restaurant or a grocery store or a movie theater, about our daughter's annoying behavior, and then got angry at ourselves for doing so. Let them just deal with it, we would say between gritted teeth to each other, and then would go out and apologize the next time she acted out. It took us years to learn to be oblivious to the prudes and scolds and busybodies of the world, and years to learn that it was okay to be angry.

For Maeve, at age seven and onward into her teens and twenties, the anxiety and anguish at Hillary's public scenes never disappeared. She could never become inured to the stares that inevitably accompanied these episodes. To pick Hillary up off the floor of a supermarket could appear to bystanders as manhandling. Quite naturally, Maeve would become secretly angry at Hillary for causing this embarrassment, and even felt as if she would like to sock her. And then, at this mere thought, she would become overwhelmed with guilt and feel as if she were a horrible person. When I appeared oblivious, Maeve would be angry at me, since I seemed indifferent to her humiliation. It was true that I had no idea of the inner torture Maeve was feeling. Nor did Denise appreciate fully how scared Maeve had become when, at some insensitive remark by some jerk, her mother was apt to get right in the face of the offender and give him a royal dressing-down.

At school Hillary's teachers worked to provide some structure and coherence to her life. To deal with her sensitivity to touch—she was "touch-averse" to "sensory input," her psychologists declared—Jean Witt took her into the therapy tank, a shallow swimming pool full of lukewarm water, cuddling her in her arms and getting her accustomed to splashes and trickles. Jean also came up with the idea of a rice bath at home, so that Hillary could have the pleasure of sifting grain through her fingers. And so we trundled off to the local Indian deli, bought a hundred-pound sack of rice, and filled a rubber play pool with it. Hap Palmer's music was the first that Hillary's ears could tolerate, and that comforting kids' music became the starting point for Hillary's love of music, a continuum that would lead her at age eighteen to be a fancier of opera and Leontyne Price.

If she was sensitive, Hillary was also stubborn. We loved it when her teachers would say, "She has a voice of her own." She also had an iron will. In her tasks she persevered with dogged determination, and she was widely admired for it. She might be vulnerable, and unable to speak, but John Wayne's true grit was no match for this tough little cookie.

Inevitably, public school loomed. This threw us into another round of high anxiety. Any change in circumstance can easily rattle the parents of handicapped children, and we were no different. Jean Witt had made real breakthroughs with Hillary. How could we ever do without her? As it happened, we did not at first have to confront this issue. Jean Witt switched schools with Hillary and became her teacher at the Stephen Knolls School in Kensington, Maryland, for her first two years there. We were ecstatic, of course, and leaped to the conclusion that our irresistibly charming child was the reason for Jean's switch of jobs.

From school we were learning a new vocabulary and a new way of thinking. When Hillary persisted in the same activity over and over, she was "perseverating." When she gurgled and chortled, she was "vocalizing." When she piled similar colored blocks one on top of another, she was improving her "motor imitation responses." We learned that she showed pleasure in "vestibular stimulation."

In due course, we were introduced to the IEP, the individualized education plan, which was customized to the "special needs" of the individual child and which set out the goals for the school year. This was a challenge. From the battery of psychological tests, with such handles as the Bailey Scale of Infant Development, the Vineland Adaptive Behavior Scales, and the Sequenced Inventory of Communication Development, all administered by bespectacled PhD psychologists, we learned that in terms of her expressive and receptive language, her self-help skills, her attention span, and her eye contact with others, Hillary had the mental age of a nine-month-old infant. Her strength was her "manipulative skill." This was no surprise to me, for she had all the feminine wiles of a coquette. Indeed, she was such a flirt that her older sister, Maeve, no slouch at flirting herself, could feel pangs of jealousy when Hillary would snuggle up on our living room couch to Maeve's latest boyfriend. (I was disappointed later to find out that to a psychologist, "manipulative skill" meant only that she was good at pegs and puzzles.)

Inevitably, some time after Hillary's near-death experience (which I will relate in the next chapter), the time for a new teacher came. Again, we were in a swivet. Not only were we getting a different teacher, but a rookie who had never taught handicapped kids before and was fresh out of school. On paper we should not have been disquieted about this new teacher, Helen Weisel, since her education had been in psychology and theology. She had nearly become a nun, and her master's degree was in the education of the profoundly handicapped. Later we would learn that Helen, like many teachers of the handicapped, was stoutly pro-life. She believes that handicapped people have just as much value as anyone else. Only when we get to heaven and see how the handicapped affect other people's lives, Helen would tell me one day, would we understand God's plan.

One look at Helen put our anxieties aside. She was a lovely, lithe young woman with a great bush of blond hair, a big smile, and a hesitant but precise way of speaking. She had brilliant green eyes and a manner so genuine, so utterly without artifice, that as denizens of a capital city so full of phonies, we shook our heads at our good fortune. She would become Hillary's Annie Sullivan.

To watch Helen in a classroom of eight needy children, with various medical problems past and present evident from their wheelchairs or helmets or body braces, was like watching a major-league sporting event with a world-class athlete. Always full of fun and creativity, yet intent to push each of her charges to their limit, she would flit around her circle with the speed of a hummingbird. By the end of class, she was often drenched in sweat. She brooked no laziness, and she was tough, so much so that she would acquire the nickname "the Warden."

She knew how to ignore the clutter and hone in on the essence. The clutter was the slurred speech or deformed hands or runny noses, the biting or the scratching or the climbing, or in Hillary's case the swings between speeded-up scatter and nearly impenetrable lethargy. The essence was the training of that mind to its fullest potential. She was good, and would get visibly excited when she watched a student grasp a concept. She derived tremendous satisfaction from her work. I admired her greatly.

Helen has no children of her own. Not infrequently, especially after Hillary moved on from her classroom years later, she would call on the occasional weekend to invite Hillary out for lunch or for an afternoon outing to the zoo or to a nearby state park. Their pleasure in each other's company was evident. Hillary would chortle her glee at the sight of Helen's spiffy silver sports car when it rolled up in the driveway in a cloud of dust. Then they would climb in the car, give each other a high five, and peel out, two birds on a fling, with Helen's hair blowing in the wind and Hillary's little mouth breaking into a mischievous smirk.

Hours later they would return. Hillary would be in peak form, sharp and lively, and very happy indeed.

Helen regaled us with hilarious tales of adventure at a duck pond or along a leafy pathway. She took great delight in Hillary's sharp attention to the cute boys they encountered along the street. Once they witnessed the feeding of the sea lions at the National Zoo, accompanied by a lecture from a prissy zookeeper about how some people actually throw coins into the sea lions' pool and how this was very bad for the animals, whereupon Hillary chose the moment to arc her water bottle into the pool with a big splash. The crowd turned in horror on the culprit, only to see upon Hillary's face a look of beatific innocence.

On another occasion when they came home in our absence, Hillary walked into her brother's second-story room, closed the door, and locked it. Noisy, insistent appeals did no good. Hearing Hillary push out the window screen, Helen feared disaster and raced outside. Hillary began to throw her brother's posters out the window. Athlete that she was, Helen knew nothing else to do but climb the chimney like Spider-Woman, using a mountain climber's finger- and toeholds, and scramble in the window.

At their leave-takings, Hillary would climb up on a window seat and put her nose to the cold glass to watch Helen's wistful departure. Many, many years after the medical crises of Hillary's early life, and long after Hillary had left her classroom, Helen was still calling to suggest a girls' night out. Though these outings certainly qualified as "child care," and gave us a needed breather, she would never take money. This was social, not business, she insisted. Once, however, after an outing and just before she was going to Italy for a month's vacation, this remarkable woman let us stake her to a gondola ride in Venice.

In the spring of 1986, we could count our blessings for the love that was lavished on Hillary in her fifth year of life. And we lavished our own love. It was at about this time, before she faced the most dangerous threat to her survival, that a report on National Public Radio arrested my attention. It was the story of an aging couple with a handicapped son who now approached his thirtieth year. They had arrived at the moment when they were no longer able physically to care for him, and he would have to be taken away. It was a wrenching tale of sorrow, for his care had become the center of their life, the source of their greatest satisfaction and happiness. Now it was no longer to be.

For families who have not experienced the presence of a handicapped child in the house, it is difficult to comprehend the joy of caring. My own parents had been after me continuously to consider institutionalizing Hillary. My mother—a graceful, charming woman who cared much about etiquette—was mortified to be with Hillary in a public place when she was misbehaving. The subject of institutionalization was taboo in our house, and my parents dared not raise it with Denise. I did not fault them, though I made it quite clear that we would never consider "putting Hillary away" until, perhaps, like the couple in the NPR report, we were incapable of managing her. Traditionalists that they were, my father and mother merely reflected the way these things were dealt with by their generation, if you were people of means.

Institutionalization rarely crossed Devin or Maeve's mind—it was so far from anything that was ever considered or discussed at home. The subject only arose occasionally with their friends, when the children spoke of all the work that the care of Hillary involved. Their friends were merely amazed, and the amazement reinforced the notion of how different our lives were from those of most other people. Our children had parents who rarely went out, given the high cost of babysitting, or if they did, they went separately. Moreover, they never complained about the sacrifices they made. That institutionalization was never considered in our house would become a point of pride for Maeve when she was older.

A number of images occurred to me about what Hillary had become to us. She was like an inflammation, raw and dangerous. Her very existence was at risk, but we, too, were at risk in a different way. We had surrounded her like scar tissue, partly for our own sakes. We sought to protect and to nurture her, to help her to thrive and to achieve whatever she would within her limits. We tried to shore up her fragile, compromised body against the many threats that lay in wait for her. She was our flesh and blood, but she was also the product of our genes. It was just possible that the very genes we had imparted to her had left her defenseless against terrible predators. We were all in this together.

She had also become the molten core of our family. We had come to revolve around her, as Earth's crust surrounds its hot, volcanic center. And because of that core, because of our vigilance against constant eruptions, we had become stronger as a unit. It was as Hemingway had written in *A Farewell to Arms:* "The world breaks everyone, then some become strong at the broken places."

CHAPTER SEVEN

[1]

In the spring of 1986, we had good reason to be hopeful. Hillary had been bumping along for about a year in what qualified as a stable condition for her. Ever so slowly we were coming to terms with her fate and ours. Driving with Miss Hillary was something like driving with Miss Daisy: We needed to be on the defensive, ever on the outlook for road hazards or reckless drivers who might sideswipe us and run us into a ditch.

Our problems were often more amusing than desperate. Sometimes they had to do with shoes. During this patch Hillary had developed an annoying penchant for untying every shoelace within reach, starting with her own. And so we bought shoes with buckles. But she found a way to unfasten them as well. In a last desperate move, Jean Witt resorted to taping her shoes so Hillary couldn't get them off, no matter what. This would, however, create a few problems in public.

For years we had been shopping for children's shoes at a neighborhood establishment called Ramer's Shoes. It is a kind of throwback to the premall days, a small shop on a byway just off Chevy Chase Circle. A tiny bell tinkles when you enter. Like many humane shop owners we had encountered along the way, Mr. Ramer, an elderly gentleman with a kindly face, was intensely interested in Hillary, and always took special care with her. As cherry blossom time approached in Washington, Denise went over to Ramer's for the annual ritual.

In the shop on that particular day was another mother with a young girl about Hillary's age. When Hillary sat down and Mr. Ramer began to lavish her with his charm, the girl turned to her mother and whispered, "Why does that little girl have tape on her shoes?" Even softer, the mother whispered back, "It's sad, so sad."

Sad, so sad? Bull. This immediately became a mantra in our household, when the least whiff of self-pity wafted into the room. "It's sad, so sad," someone would say with downcast eyes and mock pity, and then burst out in howls of laughter. Hillary's story was not sad, but triumphant. We were determined to think of it that way. When a close friend offered his sympathy once, I cut him off.

"Hillary is the soul of our family," I said.

She was going to beat this thing. She was the Unsinkable Molly Brown, the heartbeat and the heartthrob of our family. We were growing impatient with the sympathy of others, however well intentioned and sensitive, and we were discarding our own self-pity. We were entering Phase II.

Within half an hour, Mr. Ramer opened the door for our mademoiselle. His bell tinkled overhead, and Hillary bounded out onto the street in a shiny new pair of English sandals, bright red with double straps and cutouts for her cute toes. She was the cat's meow.

Down on the Mall, of Capitol fame, the cherry blossoms were in their glory as usual. The Reston brood paraded down to the Jefferson Memorial in their finery, feeling both grand and awed. Somewhere on the far side of the Tidal Basin, not far from Jefferson himself, Denise was distracted for a split second, and when she turned back to Hillary, the imp was barefoot. There in the water, surrounded by pink blossoms but no strains of Puccini's hummingbird chorus (and no haiku), were two perfect English sandals floating out among the petals . . . and then sinking. In the years afterward we could never go to see the cherry blossoms without thinking wistfully of those two perfect red shoes amid the floating blossoms.

A month later, on Mother's Day, we took off for a day in the country, in high spirits and full of spring joy. When we arrived at the cabin at Fiery Run, I went to unbuckle Hillary from her car seat and noticed that her body was strangely puffy. The seat belt was tight around her gelatin girth, and her face was bloated. In a flash Denise remembered that Jean Witt had reported puffiness in Hillary at school late in the previous week. But the condition had disappeared, and Denise had forgotten about it.

We were alarmed. Hillary was palpably heavier, so much so that Denise could scarcely lift her, and she didn't want to walk herself. Before we sprang into Code Blue, we decided on a brief walk to the stream. As we set off, we heard a terrible crashing sound and hustled down to Fiery Run to find a car horribly pinioned on a railing of the bridge and teetering precariously, as if it might tip over into the stream at any minute. In the backseat, a teenage girl was trapped in crumpled steel and screaming for help. Her sixteen-year-old sister and mother stood by the wreck, hysterical and in shock. The bridge over Fiery Run lies at the bottom of a steep grade and a sharp curve to the right. On this family foray to nearby Front Royal, the sixteen-year-old had been driving and had taken the curve too fast.

It was not a good day for mothers in the Blue Ridge. Desperately worried though she was about her own child, Denise could scarcely leave the scene, and so she spent precious time holding her balloon of a daughter with one arm and talking endlessly to the trapped girl and the shaken mother until the volunteer firemen could arrive and cut the girl safely out. Nor was it a good day for children. Maeve and Devin stood dutifully beside their mother at this horrible scene, and they would never forget it. Many years later, when he was in college, Devin would think of that girl in the backseat screaming for help as the car teetered on the brink of disaster as a metaphor for Hillary's life to come.

Within hours we were back in town and tracking down our pediatrician and lifelong friend-to-be, Dr. Paul Peebles. To him we had entrusted the whole of Hillary. Instead of impersonally sending us to the emergency room on that Sunday, Dr. Peebles arrived at our house with a battered doctor's bag and in his tennis clothes. He, too, appeared a bit shaken, and palpably downcast. His sixteen-year-old son, Gustav, he announced, had beaten him that afternoon in tennis for the first time ever. For Dr. Peebles, this marked a profound watershed, something like a benchmark toward incipient old age. His mortality yawned before him. Doctors also have their personal lives, we were discovering. How curious. How interesting. We had never thought of them that way.

Dr. Peebles immediately suspected a problem with Hillary's kidneys. Instead of sending her to the hospital, and the random crapshoot of the weekend emergency room, he advised us to wait till morning, so that Hillary could see the two best nephrologists at Children's Hospital in downtown Washington.

As the doctor drove away, Denise retreated into her private fury and her shattered faith. Over eight hours she had watched her daughter puff up to grotesque size, after three years of witnessing the destruction of Hillary's brain. So now it was the kidneys. How much worse can you make things, God, she muttered under her breath. Is there nothing more you can do to this family?

[2]

The following day, at the mirror-plated Children's Hospital in Washington, we came under the care of the two nephrologists that Dr. Peebles had recommended. Little did we know that we were beginning a relationship with Dr. Jerry Ruley and Dr. Glenn Bock that would last for fifteen years. Having received some knowledge about how the human brain worked, we now had to learn about the kidney. It was, said Dr. Bock, the stupidest of organs, nothing like the magnificent and noble brain. Its function was to filter the proteins from food and distribute them appropriately through the body. And it rid the body of poisons and toxins.

The immune system of the body mediates and affects kidney function. We thought of that separate system as the body's great defense against infection, and associated its breakdown with AIDS. The problem here was that Hillary's immune system had overreacted to the abnormalities and possibly to the toxic seizure medicines in her body. The need was to moderate this overreaction and give it a rest. It was likely that the aggressive measure to treat her seizures with ethosuximide had compromised her kidneys. No one had ever told us that was a risk.

Her condition was called minimum change nephrotic syndrome. Minimum change? We looked at our bloated child and shook our heads. Where did they get this language? But the doctors were reassuring. There was a nice, easy treatment. Only very rarely did this syndrome develop into something more complicated. The minimum change of her current bloating would soon be no change at all. We sighed our relief, and then caught ourselves. Hadn't we heard this drift somewhere before?

The antidote, said the doctors, was a medicine called prednisone. It was a steroid, and it should quiet this overzealous immune system. Here, for once, we had some acquaintance with a drug. Denise had taken prednisone in North Carolina for her allergies to all things green and dusty. But warily she remembered her Carolina doctor expressing hesitation in prescribing it. Taking prednisone, the Carolina doctor had said, was like hammering the lungs with a baseball bat.

Still, we embraced the hope of the moment: that Hillary would be back to "normal" soon.

Were there any risks? we asked. By quieting down the immune system with a powerful steroid, you can make a child more susceptible to another illness. By suppressing the immune response, you could also mask an infection.

How were we to react to that? Something had to be done and fast. Hillary was "spilling protein." Toxic fluid was collecting throughout her whole body. We were helpless to respond, much less to object. What did we know? Other infections? Like what? We were afraid to ask.

So we lugged our child home with the new poison in her medical arsenal. In the succeeding weeks, her situation remained more or less the same. She could not walk for all the excess fluid she was carrying, and we could scarcely lift her. And she was suffering. The doctors seemed mystified. In their mystification, a new theory emerged, once again a theory we were in no position to challenge or dispute. Hillary, we were told, was different. She metabolized medicines differently. If she was not improving, she must not be getting enough medicine to reach her particular magical "therapeutic level." They proposed to double the dose of prednisone.

Before they did, they took the prudent step of ordering a biopsy, just to be sure that her kidneys were not fighting some more exotic infection. The biopsy was normal—like the first CAT scan of her brain.

It was as if our Hillary had lost the center of her humanness, at least of her physical humanness. She was different, unique. We heard a constant refrain: Her case was more complicated, more confusing than that of most other human beings. The normal rules did not apply. Therefore, the prevailing thinking went, she needed twice as much of everything to gain some control. Since she was not average, the average dose was not sufficient for her.

And indeed, for a week, on her double dose of prednisone, her fluids did seem to go down.

One hot evening in July, Denise's law firm offered her free Orioles tickets, and because she is a baseball nut, and because it was a chance for a normal outing, she was tempted. I urged her to go, even though I was inordinately worried about Hillary. She did not seem herself. My worry, in turn, worried Denise, since I was somewhat more dulled to the unending drumbeat of crisis. When I worried, Denise paid attention. She went, reluctantly, with her law partner and Minnesota native, Pam Horowitz, and was glad she did, because the Orioles trounced the Twins and their ace, Frank Viola, 6–2, and both Cal Ripken and Kirby Puckett homered.

When she returned home late, Hillary still seemed to be off kilter. And so we took her into our own bed for the night, and she slept between us. With the first light, Denise turned to her child. Hillary's lips were absolutely blue.

We rushed her to Children's Hospital. In the bustle of the emergency room, she was put under an oxygen tent. Gradually, her color seemed to return. Hours went by, until somehow it was evening, and Hillary had been moved to an intermediate care unit. The doctors still did not have a handle on what was going on. As usual in these situations, I went home to tend to the needs of the other children. Inevitably, Denise's stalwart friend Pam Horowitz turned up bearing goodies and good cheer. Pam was a rock. She was always there when Denise needed her.

They chatted into the late evening by Hillary's bedside, until finally the nurses invited Pam to leave. As she and Denise stood over Hillary's bed, looking down through the plastic to her now flushed cheeks, Denise said, "Doesn't she look like a little rose."

Pam left.

Twenty minutes later Hillary's lungs collapsed.

[3]

The first thing that hits you when you enter the room is the blinding light. In the center is a large console where the doctors stand in their white coats and bark their orders. The beds are close together. Plastic is everywhere, plastic tubing, mainly, and when you look more closely, those tubes are attached to noses and necks and places in children's bodies where there are no orifices. And then gradually you hear the sounds of emergency: alarms attached to machines of every conceivable shape and size. These in turn are attached to scopes with wavy lines that calibrate the vital signs. At the foot of each bed a nurse sits, attentively monitoring every measurement and shift in body language, responding to every alarm, alerting the doctor at the console to the least sign of impending catastrophe. In the midst of this unspeakable danger, the doctors' faces are torn with fatigue and strain, their heads jerking like human periscopes to the least threat to a life. They live nonstop on the border between life and death. The intensity of the place is overwhelming.

Hillary's bed is on the far side of this intensive care unit. There are tubes in her arms and nose, a shunt in her neck. The nurse tries to explain the various monitors and fluids and medicines: for her collapsed lungs, her failed kidney, her uncontrollable seizures, the medicines to replace her flattened immune defenses. The nurse explains, but we cannot take it all in. It is too much. Too overwhelming. All around her are other desperately ill children, teetering on the edge like Hillary. It is not supposed to be this way, we think. Children are not supposed to be desperately ill, much less die.

The night is the issue—even though, in this place of obscene, dazzling light, there is no night. Will she make it through the night? That's the question. Her lungs are whitening out, we're told. A bacteria called klebsiella is racing, unchecked, through her bloodstream; pneumonia is raging through her body, and she has no immune defense to repulse it; fluid is filling her lungs. They are trying to keep ahead of the infection by draining the fluid directly from the lungs, but it's a struggle to keep ahead. They pump her with megadoses of antibiotics.

In a place of such dire situations, it's not customary for parents to be let in. There is a waiting room just outside. But its sterile couches and frantic parents are torture, worse than the intensive care unit itself. I cannot bear the separation, even of a single wall. Then, I think, I would be so lucky to wait there for a few nights. I am in a fog, in shock, in denial.

Denise, in turn, goes at the situation head-on. To the head physician, she says, "Hillary can't talk. No one can tell her what is going on. If I'm here, I can help and explain. She will know I'm there. But if I have to be next door, she won't know. She needs me. Please don't make me leave." The doctor relents. She can stay. There may be times, he says ominously, when she will be asked to leave temporarily.

For now it is the night, this night, that matters. Hillary's eyes are shut, but she is awake and in pain, for her brow is furrowed, her way of communicating her pain and her fear. Denise is in her ear, talking to her constantly for hours. Occasionally, she opens Hillary's eyes with her fingers so that the child can see, even if just a fuzzy image of her mother overhead. "Don't leave me," Denise says, as if it is a command. "Don't you dare leave me." It is an order, no excuses, meant to elicit a child's obedient response.

But in her ear is not enough. Hillary needs her mother's touch and her mother's arms to fight. She needs to feel the depth of her mother's love, palpably, immediately. A nurse named Jackie witnesses this relationship quizzically from the end of the bed. Finally, she says, "You can get up there with her."

And so, under Jackie's guidance, in the glare of klieg lights, and in the press of vulnerable humanity, Denise crawls gingerly into the ICU bed, instructed about where she can lie and where she can hold her child, tethered to the tubes and wires of life support. Entwined thus together, they cuddle through the night.

Dawn presents itself in the far shuttered window like a fake painting in a cheap hotel. And yet it is not fake. It comes up rosy and cheerful over the far trees of Catholic University, and it is the most beautiful dawn Denise has ever seen.

For the moment Hillary is resting peacefully, and Denise disentangles herself to make her way to the washroom. In the mirror she regards her ravaged face. She has been so bitter about Hillary's losses. With her child teetering on the edge, Denise had been focused on the loss of the child she initially had. That child was indeed dead. Gone forever. For three years her setbacks have been unrelieved.

Most of all, Denise has been angry at her God. She has turned away, unable to pray, for she has been unable to reconcile this situation with her concept of a benevolent God.

Now it is time to bargain.

"If you will only let my daughter live," she whispers into the mirror between clenched jaws, "I will never complain again about her being mentally retarded." Despite all Hillary's losses, her mother sees in that instant how much she has. She feels the importance of a single life, appreciates all she has left. She will never, never again measure the losses, she promises, only the gains. But let Hillary live.

It is a profound turning point.

[4]

During the midmorning, the doctors do ask Denise to leave the ICU for a short time while they remove a dead child. He had been born with a defective heart, and in the past day Denise had witnessed the torment of his parents. They had arrived the day before with balloons and soaring hope. During the night, the scream of the mother cut through the partition. Then came the invitation to enter the ICU to say good-bye, and now this finality. We understand that in a place like this not every child will make it. Intellectually, we accept that. It puts us into the mind-set of the lottery player. How can we beat the odds? We have no idea of what the odds are. To her mirror in the washroom, Denise says, "Please God, don't let it be mine."

Let us leave with the balloons.

For us that morning the action is in the hospital cafeteria. In that sterile institutional space, an area is cordoned off for the doctors. Across the room we can see Dr. Ruley and Dr. Bock in intense conversation, poring over a sheaf of pink papers. Hillary's life is now in their hands. Her numbers are on the pink slips. Pink slip? I try not to think about the analogy. We can feel their resolve across the waste-strewn tables. When we match this determination with the intensity of the ICU doctors, it is awesome to witness the medical profession gather its resources to save a life.

To save the life of a severely retarded child? In the course of this terrible weekend, we catch a whiff of the unspoken, the unspeakable horror that goes to the core of our paranoia. "Perhaps it would be for the best" had slipped out of the mouth of a doctor. "You could get on with your life." The irony was that the doctor spoke the words from a wheelchair, for he was himself handicapped. Did he speak from his own self-loathing, or at least, loathing for his own condition? How could we know what he would do in the privacy and secrecy of his craft? There were ghoulish stories about killer doctors. Doctors who play God . . . and the Devil. We had read about them in the newspapers. But he got no further before Denise turned on him with her full fury.

"If you ever, ever get close to my daughter again, I will haunt you for the rest of your life," she hissed at him. Then she threw him off the case.

Later I think of the passage from Kenzaburō Ōe's novel, *A Personal Matter*.

"They're afraid the baby will weaken and die before they can operate," Bird said . . .

"Well that's probably for the best!" the young doctor replied.

The hope, the scream, the goodbye, the disposal and finality. . . . and then the grief and perhaps eventually the reconciliation. Perhaps it would be for the best.

"Some people have a funny way of being optimistic about this kind of case, but it seems to be the quicker the infant dies, the better for all concerned. I don't know, maybe it's the difference in generations. I was born in 1935. How about you?"

"Somewhere around there. I wonder if it's suffering."

"What, our generation?"

"No, the baby!"

"That depends on what you mean by suffering. I mean, the baby can't see or hear or smell, right? And I bet the nerves that signal pain aren't functioning, either. It's like the Director said, you remember, a kind of vegetable. In your opinion, does a vegetable suffer?"

Perhaps it will be best if I could adopt Ōe's existential view. Why not be pessimistic? If she dies, it will be expected, and I will be prepared. The shock and personal pain will be less. I can get on with my life. If a death is expected, the grieving period might be just as intense, but wouldn't it be shorter in duration? I have been to only one funeral of a child in my life. I remembered how the parents looked almost . . . well . . . saintly.

I cannot bear more crushed hope. Perhaps there is no purpose to this world after all. Perhaps Denise is talking in that mirror only to her own image. Perhaps there is no value to Hillary's life. We have heard that one before, too. "There are valuable people and less valuable people," Brecht had written, putting the words in the mouth of the Jewish wife faced with the Nazi extermination. Hadn't the Nazis gassed the handicapped? For the purity of the race. Was the indiscreet, chairbound, MS-suffering doctor really being sensitive? As a handicapped person himself, perhaps he can only imagine that our life will be hell if Hillary lives. He has no conceivable notion of the joy she brings to us. If he and other doctors really think that way, how do we know they are doing everything they can to save her?

Early on Sunday morning, Dr. Peebles shakes me on the couch of the ICU waiting room. It is not looking good, he says. Her lungs are still whiting out. He takes Denise and me into a side room. Institutional white. Mock wood chairs and a Formica table. So banal. So ordinary. So this is how it happens. He doesn't think she's going to make it. If anybody wants to say good-bye, they should get in here right away.

Is this really happening?

What about the children? Dr. Peebles leaves it up to them. To them? A seven-year-old and a five-year-old? Well, to us and them. Sometimes, he says, when children never get to say good-bye, it will haunt them later. They might not be able to put it behind them.

In a blur, family materializes from everywhere. Denise's family from New York; my brother from Massachusetts. I can't remember how they got here. My parents are there, too. I cannot talk to them and ask Dr. Peebles to do so. He pulls them aside.

"Why don't you just let her go?" my father says to the doctor.

I make one call outside the family, to the only friend I have who himself has a handicapped child.

"I don't know if I can get through this . . . ," I begin, and I don't.

Maeve and Devin arrive, wide-eyed, shell-shocked. At some point in the chaos, Dr. Peebles spirits them into a side room alone. Again, I have lost my nerve. I should do this, but I leave it to him. He's the professional. I'm an amateur at death speeches. To them this doctor, with his brush mustache and his ruddy hair and his ready smile, has always been a source of comfort, but now that face is etched with a sadness even a five-year-old can recognize. They know that something is very wrong. Hillary is very,

very sick. She has a fifty-fifty chance, he says softly. If she gets better, she will be home. If she does not make it, she can fall into a sleep for many years. She can fall so deeply asleep that no one will be able to wake her. Hillary will always be with us. She will be at home in your heart and in your head. And you will always be able to talk to her there, in your heart, in your head, at home.

We take them in to see Hillary. They stand silent and stiff beside her bed, overwhelmed by all the machinery and by the ghostly look of their sister. What a thing we are asking them to do. They do not know what to say. Hillary lies there, tubes and wires coming out of everywhere, eyes shut, brow furrowed, whitening out.

"She looks like a robot," Devin says.

Not a nice thing to say, we scold.

[5]

As she lies next to her child, Denise drifts in a surreal dreamland. It is as if she is again on the bed where she gave birth to Hillary. It is December 1981 again, and Hillary is not six years but only six hours old. The mother enfolds her newborn in her arms. She can hear the voice of Dr. Silverman in the distance. "What a strong baby!" the doctor is saying in her Hungarian accent, as Hillary lifts her head off Denise's chest briefly. She is such a rag doll, so fragile. Denise is afraid to press too hard, and yet the child must feel the love. She imparts life flow. She has a mother's power. Her life energy is transferring.

She hears another voice. But this one is here, close by, immediate, and it snaps her out of her reverie. It is Monday morning already, and the voice comes from the Israeli doctor who has been hovering over Hillary's case in the ICU for the past forty-eight hours. She looks up at his exhausted face. She's not getting any worse, he is saying about Hillary. Her lungs did not white out anymore in the night. What did it mean?

"She has a shot," he says.

For the next two days, Hillary takes her shot. Her lungs might be white; her kidneys may have failed; she might have terrible brain seizures, and stress ulcers from the ICU. But she takes her shot anyway. She has a reputation to uphold.

On Wednesday the Israeli doctor shakes Denise again. His face looks better. He'd had some sleep. He holds his fists up in exultation.

"She's gonna make it!" he says.

When he's gone, Denise turns to Hillary.

"When we get out of here, kid, we're going to Disney World!" They had just won the Super Bowl, the Olympics, the World Series. And then: "We did it! . . . No. . . . You did it!" And she, too, holds her fists up in the air in triumph, the way she would years later when the Mets made it into the World Series. This was one world-class performance.

Ten days later we leave with balloons. The Israeli doctor walks us out. How can we thank him? And we go to

Disney World, where we get a room for $99 next to the Michael Jackson Suite. At breakfast the first day in Florida, Hillary eats four Danishes.

In the smallest things, we take immense, stratospheric pleasure.

Part II

QUALITY OF LIFE

CHAPTER EIGHT

By 1990, five years after Hillary's brush with death, we had reached the limit of our wits and our skill.

Her small store of energy had become positively thermonuclear. During the day she could be nearly comatose for hours, and then she would explode with the most dangerous acts. She was an Olympian climber with no sense of danger. She clambered on windowsills, onto the top of kitchen cabinets, onto ledges and precipices. She had begun to swallow tiny objects she found on the floor. Staples, LEGOs, even tacks began to appear in her stool. To gain attention she banged a cup with atomic force. Glass especially seemed to attract her. With a single blow she severed a heavy round glass-topped dining table, and in horror I watched its two halves fall harmlessly on either side of her spindly legs. In restaurants she bit through water glasses, an impulsive act that led to our frantically scooping out her mouth to be sure we had all the pieces. She totaled so many glass panes in our house that we cut a special after-hours deal with our local glazier as he looked at us askance and replaced the twentieth pane with Plexiglas. Once she somehow found a glass beer mug and smashed it onto the side of her bathtub, cutting herself and making the bathwater run red with blood.

By necessity we all had to develop a sixth sense about her whereabouts. Hillary's whole being seemed to be devoted to escaping whatever constraints were placed upon her. But it was an inexact science. Frequently, she outwitted us, and we began to call her the Great Houdini. To contain her, we installed an elaborate system of locks and latches to fence her in and keep her in bounds. It did not always work. On one occasion Maeve found her on the roof of my porch, high above the ground, after she had climbed out a second-story window. Hills had done this out of spite and female annoyance, I suspected, because I was down in the basement, absorbed in a Redskins football game, and her mother was at work on a Sunday.

But the worst moment came when Denise was away. Devin was sleeping peacefully upstairs, and I broke a cardinal rule of the household. In an apparently serene and settled domestic scene, I left Hillary in her room, bolting the front door, and then zipped a half mile away to pick up the babysitter. The bad luck came in the form of a broad-shouldered West Virginia logger with a load of fire-wood who banged on the front door during this brief absence and woke up the sleeping children. Devin, droopy-eyed and unaware that I was not there, answered the door, sent the man packing, and slid blissfully back between the sheets without rebolting the door. When I turned onto our street twenty minutes later with the babysitter, I saw, to my horror, a somnambulant and bare-foot Hillary heading directly for the fast-moving traffic of Wisconsin Avenue. Before I could get to her, she turned right on the sidewalk, as if guided by some providential force, instead of walking straight out into the busy thoroughfare.

Quietly, I piled her in the car and took her home, wondering how many sets of Kew Garden eyes had looked through their shutters, seen her striding toward disaster unattended, and done nothing on that long two-block walk to the boulevard. I was too mortified at my lapse to tell Denise.

In my guilt I remembered a story told to me by a great friend of mine in my early writing career, a South Carolina novelist, Elizabeth Coker. Elizabeth was the mother of a Carolina classmate, the estimable James Lide Coker IV, and she lived along an elegant moss-covered street in Hartsville, South Carolina. From time to time, her neighbor (I will call her Mrs. Ballinger) would take off all her clothes and sashay onto Main Street buck naked. Without fail some-one would rush to her—sometimes it was Elizabeth—throw a blanket around her, and gently take her home.

She was just Mrs. Ballinger, a harmless curiosity on the small-town landscape. No one seemed to mind, and no one talked about "putting her away." It was just life in Hartsville. Mrs. Ballinger was a person like everyone else; indeed, quite an interesting person. I remembered the story at that moment, no doubt, to shift attention away from my own negligence. How different the small-town South was from the suburbs of Washington.

Over the years there would be a score of these mistakes. We all made them, and Hillary did not always escape the consequences. Her body still bears some of the scars. When we faulted ourselves, we would return to something another of Hillary's doctors, her pediatrician, Dr. Paul Peebles, had once said to us about the inevitability of accidents: "Don't guilt yourself." Easy for him to say, I thought. It was the only time I ever heard *guilt* used as a verb.

Even with her seizures coming under control, Hillary remained without language, without the barest sense of danger and caution, and without the most basic skills of a one-year-old. She did not achieve potty training until she was nine years old, meaning that together with our other two children, we experienced thirteen years of diapers. To take her out in public was always an adventure. Her "vocalizations," as the doctors called her language, qualified more as screams and shrieks to normal people, and at their most shrill often presaged an imminent seizure. Occasionally, her yelps in public could take an amusing turn.

Once we boarded a public bus in Washington, and I noticed an apparently homeless man sleeping peacefully a few seats behind us. Just as we sat down, Hillary let out a blood-curdling yelp. The homeless man startled and sat up.

"Who said that?" he demanded. "That's exactly right!"

This became our family joke for ever after when Hillary shouted out.

"Who said that? That's exactly right!"

For a child to have a brain seizure in a public restaurant, however, is only one step removed on the panic scale from a fire in a packed theater. This made the "dining experience" more than awkward for both us and those around us. As the writer who has labored alone for decades, I have always considered myself to be an invisible man. I see everything, but no one sees me. Public incidents with Hillary did not affect me as much as they did Denise and the children. What will people think? The phrase had been a mantra of my childhood. Now the challenge was to learn not to care.

We had long since become accustomed to being watched in public. Quite apart from normal curiosity, watching us was a good idea for those around us. Hillary was in her knife-throwing stage. To the casual diner at the next table, it could be disconcerting, not to mention downright dangerous, to see a knife go whizzing by his head . . . then to turn around and see the very face of angelic innocence on the little girl at the next table.

Still, the problem of the restaurant gave rise to one of

the most famous Hillary stories in our family repertoire. Inevitably, the scene took place when I was away, and Denise was alone with the children in Ocracoke, North Carolina, for needed sun and rest. At one of our favorite haunts at the beach, Hillary was being horrid—loud, throwing spoons, trying to escape her chair—while the other two children, in their embarrassment, were not much better behaved. Somehow Denise made it through the meal without bursting into tears. When she marched her naughty children to the counter to pay the bill, the cashier announced in her sweetest Elizabethan brogue that the bill had already been paid . . . by the gentleman across the room who had been dining alone and who had just left. Vaguely, Denise remembered taking notice of a man with a beard in a far corner of the restaurant. Forever after, he entered our hall of heroes as the Great Bearded Benefactor, and we're still searching for him twenty years later. Accustomed as we were to people seeing and pretending not to see, he had seen and had done his part for humanity, anonymously, charitably, and we were grateful.

On other occasions we found ourselves trying to calm down bystanders to Hillary episodes. Once, during the inevitable annual trip to Disney World, the family was dining in the French Pavilion at the Epcot Center, which is modeled after a Paris café. Our waitress, a teenage exchange student from Paris, contributed to the ambience. After the meal our waitress was collecting the dessert plates, and Hillary was drinking water, when the rascal bit her glass and a large chip of it fell on the table. The waitress turned deathly white and started babbling frantically in French. After we made sure that Hillary had not cut herself—she had not—Devin attended to the waitress.

"That's just our Hillary," he said reassuringly, "tough as nails and chompin' on glass."

What was in Hillary's mind during these chaotic episodes? I was fascinated to know and bedeviled by not knowing. What could it feel like for a person to be always out of control? How did it feel when one felt a seizure coming on? Could she anticipate anything, or did she live entirely in the moment? She could not tell us. In this very inability to communicate her pains or worries to her own parents, there had to be an unbearable frustration. We had very little insight into these questions. For so long, we and her doctors had regarded her as an ill child and were always preoccupied with the search for a way to make her well. There was no time, it seemed, to ponder the whole person.

On what a seizure felt like, I got a partial answer from the novelist Gwyn Hyman Rubio when I sat next to her one year at the Kentucky Book Fair. As a child, Rubio had suffered with seizures, and she was eloquent now in describing them. "When a seizure is coming on," she said between signing copies of her novel *Icy Sparks,* "there is an 'aura,' a fuzzy feeling accompanied by flashing lights and odd smells. When the storm itself comes, you move out of your body, and it is as if you are looking down on yourself from the ceiling. Afterward, there is no memory of pain or shuddering."

It was hard to be Hillary.

We had dodged so many bullets. But disaster loomed. We had no way to scold or discipline her, no way to impart a sense of caution or to make her aware of the sharp edges or high cliffs that could maim or kill her.

Dr. Conry greeted our terror and exasperation with a proposal. Hillary should apply for admission to the Kennedy Krieger Institute at Johns Hopkins Hospital in Baltimore.

For the brain-damaged child, Kennedy Krieger is Harvard and Oxford in one. Founded in 1937 and originally devoted to the treatment of cerebral palsy, this prominent square building across the street from the Johns Hopkins dome has developed a world-class reputation for its creative and tough-minded approach to brain disorders in children. Two things are central to the Kennedy Krieger credo. The first is early intervention: It is critical to get a brain-damaged child at an early age if her potential is to be maximized later. And second, the child, no matter how severely brain damaged, must learn to do things for herself.

But did Hillary qualify? Were her grades bad enough, her behavior "severe" enough, to beat the rest of the desperate competition? We went to Baltimore with all the anxiety that I remembered from my own Harvard admission interview thirty years earlier. To our pleasure, Hillary was on her worst behavior. She got in, early admission.

She was headed for the vaunted Severe Behavior Unit of such international fame. The unit itself was no more than a large open space with couches in the middle and beds for the patients along the walls, and padded rooms off to the side. It was dormitory, classroom, and eating hall all in one. For the next four months, the SBU was home for Hillary and twenty other desperate cases. To look at the others was to count one's own blessings.

We had never been separated from our girl before, and this was a tug. As a result, one or the other of us made the trip to Baltimore nearly every evening to be sure that our nine-year-old did not feel that she had been abandoned. We quickly learned that our "separation anxiety" was greater than hers. We would arrive to find her engaged in happy games, puzzle solving, and boisterous guitar concerts with her handlers. She greeted our arrival without much enthusiasm, as if we were grown-ups who had come to spoil the party. What we did not fully appreciate was that it was Maeve and Devin who felt abandoned. Sullenly, they endured the explanation that if we did not go up every day, Hillary might feel that we had given up on her. This problem was alleviated a bit when we began to take Devin and Maeve along with us to Baltimore.

A day at Kennedy Krieger was all business. For the first two months, we were invited to stay away as her therapists developed their relationship with her. They observed her continuously and took their "data" relentlessly. What made Hillary tick? Why did she scream? What pleased her in eating LEGOs or other small, dangerous objects on the floor, which in the psychological lingo was called "pica"? Pica, it turned out, was considered a formal disorder. While well recognized in the trade, it had, so far, not been effectively treated. Hillary's case of it was among the worst they had ever seen at Kennedy Krieger.

The padded rooms off the unit were the classrooms. In them her therapists devised situations to simulate the dangerous objects that she was ingesting from a floor or the ground: The rocks became rock candy, slivers of paper substituted for glass, rice represented staples, water was colored to look like acid. By simulating the look of dangerous objects and allowing Hillary to ingest the innocuous items, they could test Hillary's likes and dislikes and probe her reasons for putting them in her mouth. They "baited" the room with M&M's and other "preferred items," and set up tests in which these would be given as rewards after she performed set tasks. They placed her favorite foods on a plate and a place mat, and other items on the floor, praising her when she ate appropriately and analyzing her behavior when she took something from the floor. It was the early days of the laptop computer. Her handlers sat behind mirrored glass and typed endlessly, then constructed their models and their graphs.

The child who had always had help at her beck and call was suddenly being asked to do most everything for herself. "Hillary, you do it!" became the mantra. If she did not do "it"—dressing or feeding herself, for example—the therapists were tough and patient, as if they were telling her that they could wait all day. This could result in a real test of wills.

To perform a desired task, the philosophy of the unit was "three-step guided compliance." Hillary's hearing was tested and found to be normal. No one was sure how much language she understood now. She certainly recognized the sound of her name. She recognized a negative like no, especially when it was enunciated with passion. The problem was that passionate rebukes amused her, and she would giggle or look coy when she was scolded. It was a fail-safe way of getting attention.

And so the first step of the three was verbal: "Hillary, pick up the magazine." If she did not move, the second step was to point to the magazine. And finally, if this did not work, the magazine would be given to her. Three-step guided compliance covered a wide range of activity, including eating. The procedure has become central to our care of Hillary ever since, and central to her education in school.

Communicating requests and demands was a two-way street. As a system evolved for letting her know what we wanted, she advanced her own communication system. She had been at Kennedy Krieger for no more than a few days before her "team" of PhD psychologists appreciated that this was one cunning, stubborn, and determined little girl. She had no difficulty in communicating her desires, and she did so with such force and definiteness that there could be no misinterpretation. In the wake of the Reagan presidency, we began to refer to her as "the Great Communicator." For things she didn't like, she could push you away with a sound and a look that would make Rita Hayworth envious. The team saw immediately that, in the words of the director of the SBU, Dr. Patricia Kurtz, there was a "major personality in there, a unique individual" who was determined to shape the world around her to her liking. That worldview had to be bent and altered now, maybe in a way not to her liking. This was no easy task.

Padding covered the pillars in the unit as well. This was for "consequenting." Consequenting unacceptable behavior was the last resort at Kennedy Krieger; positive reinforcement for good behavior was preferred. But we needed the last resort—and how. When the patients acted out, which was often, a therapist took them to the pillar as if it were the woodshed for a "time-out." Their hands would be pulled across their body from behind in a "basket hug," and they would be pressed snugly against the padding for sixty seconds or so. We began to see a glimmer of hope for a humane way to scold.

This was, of course, behavior modification in its purest form. Despite the popular association with electric shock or medication or surgery in the Cuckoo's Nest, the inducement to different, more-acceptable, and manageable behavior here was pain-free, drug-free emphasis on the positive.

Almost three months into her hospitalization, with her team still taking data, I began to get nervous. What were they learning? When were they going to institute a treatment plan? What method of consequenting seemed most effective? I was told to relax. Everything in its good sweet time.

What I did not appreciate was that the final treatment plan for Hillary had been evolving for some time. Not only Hillary, but her parents and her teachers as well, had to be considered in this final plan. It would be they who would implement it. Were they up to it? For one thing, fathers of cute daughters are notorious softies.

For weeks toward the end, the team had been testing various techniques to see what methods were most effective in decreasing Hillary's specific dangerous behaviors. This, then, was the reason for their endless data taking. They were measuring their success or failure. Only when they were sure of their plan did they "drop it on the unit" for all to employ. And only in the last days would we hear what they had decided.

CHAPTER NINE

[1]

Kennedy Krieger's entrance is right across the street from the emergency room for the entire Johns Hopkins medical complex, although the two institutions are separate, distinct entities. Nurses were always present in the unit, and doctors trooped through the rooms regularly. And so we found ourselves with a golden opportunity to get a thorough medical workup for Hillary at the world's finest hospital while she pursued her Harvard education. Perhaps we could, at long last, get some answers to this insidious no-name disease that had so devastated our girl.

Well into Hillary's stay, the chief medical investigator

in her case collared us in the hallway. Upon the review of her entire record, he said, they had concluded that in the gruesome spring of 1983, during those five days of high fevers in Brooklyn, Hillary had had a stroke. The idea was so simple, so clear, that in the shock of realization we wondered again how this possibly could have been missed at the time. It ran through Denise's mind for the thousandth time what she had told the Park Avenue doctor: There was something profoundly different about Hillary's aspect in those febrile days.

At the critical point in the conversation, the doctor turned to Denise and said of these five days in May, six years before, "You mean with those high fevers, she wasn't put in the hospital? . . . And you've never done anything about it!"

It was the closest we ever came to hearing one doctor suggest we should sue another.

In the medical encyclopedia, a stroke is defined as a hemorrhage in the brain that can cause a sudden loss of consciousness and subsequent paralysis. It is often caused by a lack of blood flow to the brain. This now became the operating hypothesis for the onset of Hillary's condition, and it would hold for us over the next ten years. It was a simple understandable point: that Hillary's high temperatures in those five days had interrupted the blood flow to her brain and damaged significant portions of her brain, including her language center. An MRI showed the destruction graphically.

After the shock of this explanation came the relief. What happened to her when she was two? people had always asked. Oh, we could now say, she had a stroke. People would nod their understanding. Oh, I see. For the years that we had no useful handle, Denise had often looked at Hillary and imagined opening up her skull, grabbing hold of this evil scourge as if it were a nest of snakes, and yanking it out with all her might. Now at last, with the diagnosis of stroke, this fantasy left her.

We learned ten years later, as had happened to us in the past, that stroke is a general rather than a specific term. It is not a diagnosis, any more than encephalitis (which simply means brain disease) was a diagnosis. A descriptive term only, a stroke could apply to any number of bad germs that might have generated the insult to her brain. And the insult itself might have come from some underlying process that remained undiscovered and nameless. Moreover, the "language center," we learned later, was not something that might be blown up by a terrorist bomb, like Grand Central Station. To the contrary. Language, at the stage of its formation, is fragile. It can not be destroyed in five minutes, but if the blood flow is shortened for an extensive time, say five days, the damage can be extensive. Indeed, it can.

Hillary's first stint at Kennedy Krieger transformed her life and ours. When she emerged after four months, she could nearly dress herself. She was potty trained and attentive to her surroundings. With her greatly improved attention span, she was open to instruction as never before. Most of all, we had, at last, a method for imparting to her our displeasure with her dangerous or impulsive behaviors.

To the normal person with average children, these might seem to be minor achievements for four months of intensive training. To us they amounted to a sea change. We began to sense the possibilities of the future: a relationship based upon more than blocking her off from danger. At last, life was going to be more than merely getting through the day without disaster. We could savor the thought of an openness and a curiosity and a promise of healthy adventure. The sound of shattering glass or the apparition of Hillary perched like a Cheshire cat amid the pottery on top of our kitchen cabinets ceased to be a regular occurrence.

To use old Army parlance, her transition back into "the world" was carefully orchestrated. For her first four nights at home, her Kennedy Krieger therapist was her houseguest. We gave Michelle Sherer a rocking chair, but she spent most of the night hovering upright secretly in a dark corner, waiting for Hillary to stir and to bound out of bed against the rules. And if she did, she got "the treatment."

In the field of behavioral psychology, the treatment was termed "contingent demands." It called for an acrobatic wrestler's hold from the rear, whereby the therapist (or the parent or the sibling) would grab her hands and push them to various parts of her body, describing each step flatly, without anger or irritation: "Touch your head . . . touch your nose . . . touch your chin . . . touch your waist . . . touch your feet . . ." It was performed very fast, always in the same way, for thirty seconds.

The duration was important, since, according to our experts, this length of time exhausted Hillary's attention on her transgression. Longer was both counterproductive and cruel. Hillary clearly hated the business, and it worked very well in discouraging a repeat of her naughty act. At first she resisted, but eventually she acquiesced stoically, simply waiting for the thirty seconds to elapse. But she got the point, and we shouted our hurrahs.

At school, Helen Weisel was thrilled with these new tools. At last she could be an educator again, rather than a cop on the beat. She could spend more time on Hillary's learning and expend less effort on keeping her out of trouble. In the classroom setting, however, giving Hillary the business could be disruptive. If the pupil was having a bad day, frequent episodes of contingent demands could be exhausting for the teacher, even for Helen, who was such a schoolhouse athlete. In due course, in consultation with Kennedy Krieger, Helen changed the technique to a procedure we came to know as "the face wipe." When Hillary was bad, she would get her face wiped for 30 seconds. This face touching was equally distasteful to her, and just as effective. And it was much less arduous on us all.

[2]

Seven years later, in 1997, Hillary returned to Kennedy Krieger for a second tour. I liked to think of this return engagement as graduate work. But it was more like an alcoholic's refresher course after falling off the wagon. In this second hospitalization, she was a very different girl. She was seventeen years old, a blossoming, sometimes pouty, often chipper teenager who came packaged in an eight-year-old body.

The issues were far different as well. After her brush with death thirteen years earlier, her kidneys went gradually, steadily downhill until they failed completely in 1993. From that point forward, our nightly ritual of dialysis began. The demise of her kidneys had robbed her body of its power to grow, since a central function of that otherwise stupid organ is to process protein and distribute this miraculous life force through the entire system.

After her kidneys failed, she had been on nightly peritoneal dialysis. This is a relatively new process, historically speaking; it has only been widely available in America since the 1970s. Before that time, only a small number of patients were fortunate enough to receive a rudimentary form of dialysis in the hospital. Doctors routinely had to make hard calls about which of their kidney patients would live and who would die.

Dialysis changed our lives dramatically once again. Every evening at about 9:30 p.m. we began our ritual of preparing Hillary for bed. A tube had been surgically implanted in her belly. It protruded from her stomach about twelve inches and was tipped with a catheter, or connector. Because the line went directly into her stomach, and the fluid it conducted became part of her bodily fluids, we had to be extremely careful that it never became compromised or contaminated; the consequences of that were dire. In an elaborate antiseptic routine in which we wore masks and scrubbed with special soap, we attached her gingerly to her lifeline. That line connected to a machine cradling plastic bags of viscous dialysis fluid. In five "exchanges" over approximately eight hours, during which (hopefully) she slept, this fluid cleansed her system of its toxins the way her working kidneys used to do. No one ever told us, until I learned it by chance years later, that dialysis replicates about 15 percent of normal kidney function.

Dialysis complicated our already complicated life immensely. Given the exaction of the process and the dire consequence of any mistake, the household needed military discipline to cope. I tried to make light of this necessity, invoking my military experience. I became "First Shirt"; Denise became "First Skirt"; Maeve became "Miniskirt"; and Devin became "First Shorts." Hillary became "First Diaper." (Our Irish Setter, Dara, became "First Alert," because her finely tuned sonar sometimes alerted us to the advent of a seizure before we saw it coming.)

If Hillary was fortunate to have needed the therapy when it had become widely available, we were fortunate for a technical advance that came on line only a few months after her dialysis began. At first, a massive machine looking something like a miniature oil derrick was delivered to Hillary's second-story bedroom. With daunting dials and hooks, it stood over six feet tall and clearly weighed a ton. Its massive size meant, perforce, that we would never again be able to travel with Hillary. I tried to be jolly about it at first, as I looked at her derrick and asked Hillary if she was ready for her "oil change." But I was not pleased at the notion of being a prisoner of Washington for the rest of my life.

Only a few months later, however, the white coats came to collect their oil derrick and replaced it with a fax machine–size device weighing about thirty pounds, which came with a handy carrying case and a zipper compartment for all the accessories. Instead of inhuman dials and hooks, it had buttons in forest green and magenta and a talking message board that instructed us digitally: "turn me off" or "connect yourself," along with a pleasant jingle. We dubbed it "the kid." Since that time Hillary and the kid have been to Wyoming and Florida, Nova Scotia and her spiritual home in Ireland, with only minor snafus.

The kid, however, has a shrill alarm. Whenever there was an interruption in the life flow, from air or a kink or worse, the machine squawked, and we came running. Over these years alarms in the night became a regular feature of life with Hillary. Restive in the night, she was often out of bed, banging at the bathroom door or sniffing at her air conditioner. She had learned that an alarm would bring us instantly, and she liked that. To get the alarm, she needed only to throw the bags of dialysis fluid on the floor.

What she had not learned was that if her dialysis line was compromised by exposing the fluid to the germ-filled air, she would contract peritonitis. This dread disease of the stomach spreads rapidly, and if not clobbered with antibiotics immediately can kill her. For a while 3 a.m. seemed to be her preferred time to disconnect herself. We would stumble bleary-eyed down the stairs and to find her standing, buck naked and confused in the middle of her room, with dialysis fluid gushing from her stomach onto the floor. This meant a fast search for clamps in the midden of her bathroom, frantic calls, and a race to the hospital in Virginia, where a grumpy nurse would shake her head once again and say, "Hillary, you are really sumptin!"

Even worse was her penchant for biting her line. When she bit it through, as she did on a few occasions, the germs from her mouth went into the fluid in her stomach, and the resulting peritonitis was especially virulent. When she had the condition in extremis, the infection bent her over with such pain that she walked like an old woman. We tried everything. We tried coating the line with pepper sauce, but she found that tasty. We wrapped the line with towels and plastic coils, but she found a way to defeat that. A papooselike restraint was suggested, but to me, it smacked of a straitjacket and we could not bear to think of our child as a mental case. I developed insomnia listening for her footfall on the floor.

Once again we had come to the limit of our wits and skills. We were warned that if she got too many cases of peritonitis, it could scar her peritoneum to the point that dialysis would no longer work.

Once again, Kennedy Krieger rode to the rescue.

For this second tour, her case officer was a lovely, powerful, football-playing young woman named Maureen van Stone, who, like so many other therapists at Kennedy Krieger, was getting some practical experience while she worked toward her master's in psychology at Johns Hopkins University. Maureen had just joined the staff, but after the wonderful experience with Hillary's teacher, Helen Weisel, we were no long wary of rookies. If we were not wary, Maureen herself was terrified. Hillary, she was told, was the favorite of Dr. Patricia Kurtz, Maureen's boss and the head of the unit, and Trish would be watching Maureen's every move.

The mission for the second tour was twofold: how to stop her from biting her dialysis line, and how to break this dangerous habit of dropping down like a sack of potatoes whenever she objected to a demand. The first habit was a threat to her life; the second had made our family life intolerable. Diminutive in stature though she was, Hillary made up for it in watery bulk: She now weighed about eighty pounds. For years Denise had been lifting this bloated child, and inevitably had strained her back severely. Hillary sensed this vulnerability immediately and took advantage of it. Like her father, she was an opportunist.

It had become nearly impossible for Denise to take her on errands. In the grocery store, Hillary was apt to drop down somewhere near the cereal display. Unable to budge her, the frazzled mother pushed and pulled and scolded, trying to pick up a protesting Hillary off the floor, as nosy shoppers converged joyously on the scene to accost Denise, and to berate her for abusing her poor child. This mayhem usually ended with tears and arguments, and with the store manager adjudicating and calling for the forklift.

A variation of this grocery store happening came to be known as the yapping shopper scene. Occasionally, we would find ourselves serenely in the supermarket checkout line, warmly listening to Hillary's happy little chortles and yips, only to have some wit say, looking to the ceiling in mock confusion and with great appreciation at his own woolly sense of humor, "Is there a dog in here? I think I hear a dog."

There are, no doubt, a number of even wittier ripostes that one can imagine in this situation. But murder was usually on our mind. Maeve and Devin were moving into their teens, and they reacted differently to these insensitive remarks in public. While Maeve cringed with embarrassment, Devin reacted with fury. Still slender and wispy, he wished for the build of a football player and imagined a stranglehold. Once in a restaurant, when Hillary was acting out, and a busybody across the room gawked at her, Devin stuck his tongue out at the old biddy. He had compensated for his slender stature with a sharp tongue and an endless supply of schoolyard insults.

"She's not imitating a dog, penis breath," he said once at one of these dog remarks. "She's making those pained sounds after looking at your face!" Now it was time for me to cringe with embarrassment and flee for the door.

These emergencies at the grocery store were bad enough. But what if she dropped down in the middle of a busy street?

As with so many professionals we had encountered over the course of Hillary's lifetime, we had to learn a new language at Kennedy Krieger, the language of the behavioral psychologist. The goal for this second admission, we were told, was "to conduct a stimulus choice assessment to identify potential reinforcers for Hillary." They proposed to "conduct functional analysis to determine which, if any, environmental variables maintain Hillary's maladaptive behavior."

Translated, this meant weeks and weeks of observing Hillary in the dead of night, as she might attempt to bite her dialysis line, and weeks of head scratching about how to teach her a constructive and appropriate alternative to dropping down in public.

In this hothouse of behavioral modification, the medical director held sway over all tests and procedures; safety took precedence over everything else. Because Hillary was so "medically involved," he overruled any possibility that Hillary would have direct "access" to her actual dialysis line. And so her team devised a fake dialysis tube, identical in appearance to the actual line and attached with tape to her stomach. Then the lights were turned out, and the laptop computers were switched on, and the therapists waited eagerly in the dark for Hillary to go for the fake line. The tools of "functional analysis" stood ready to document every instance of "mock tube bite" and to analyze whether the occurrence seemed to be for the purpose of gaining attention or for the sensuous gratification of a good chew.

Hillary ignored this trickery altogether. She ignored it in the first week, and in the first month. They tried giving her a "placebo tube" to bite and actually putting it past her lips. She pushed it away contemptuously. She knew a fake when she saw it. So totally disinterested in the dialysis line or the fake or placebo lines was she that we all concluded after a few months that she had simply lost interest in this dangerous mischief. The problem, we hoped, had been resolved naturally on its own. Perhaps she had grown out of it. But Hillary had a trick or two of her own. In her second night home from the hospital, we were roused by an alarm, and rushed down to find her biting her line.

Her willful acts of dropping down required far greater creativity. Here, her team spent weeks in evaluating the source of this behavior. Was she trying to gain attention, or to get things she wanted, or merely trying to escape demands? After scores of sessions, which produced a blizzard of data, Maureen and her crew concluded that escape from demands was her primary motivation. Brilliant, I thought to myself. I could have told them that. But as a father, I also knew that Hillary often felt lousy. It was no wonder that she had very little energy for outings in the neighborhood.

What to do? The team began to experiment with intervals of walk and rest, as they blocked her from dropping down on the floor. At first, the walk might last no more than a minute or two. At a local hunting store, Maureen found a camouflage hunter's stool, made of lightweight aluminum and canvas. Soon enough the team was taking Hillary to the local supermarket, demanding that she walk around for a few minutes, and then sit appropriately on her hunter's stool. In time a communication card was added, which was stuck to Velcro and hung around her neck. When Hillary was ready for a rest, she was to take the card off, hand it to her minder, and thus gain access to the stool for a rest. To reinforce this, a fanny pack stuffed with M&M's and Gummy Bears was added, so that she could communicate her desire to sit and be rewarded or reinforced with her preferred candy.

And thus Hillary lurched, however slowly and unevenly, toward "adaptive" and appropriate behavior.

[3]

Our deliverance from the nightmare of nightly dialysis was the hope for a kidney transplant. Eagerly, we placed Hillary on the Virginia transplant list not long after her kidneys failed. Her wait would be a few years, we were told, perhaps three at the most. When the wait reached three years, we got no kidney, but we did get a beeper.

And it buzzed with some regularity, because the number was one digit away from the local pizza delivery service.

In 1997 Hillary was "offered" a kidney that seemed to have all the right indicators. But it was "nicked" in the harvesting, and therefore rendered unsound. The parents of a child who had died in a tragic horseback-riding accident had, in their grief, specifically requested that the organs of their dead child go to a needy child. What must they have felt, I wondered, when on top of all else, the last vestige of life in their child had been snuffed out on the surgeon's butcher block. Much as I longed for Hillary's transplant, I could not bear to think about this grotesque connection between tragedy and new life. But we all enthusiastically listed ourselves as organ donors on our driver's licenses.

Waiting for a transplant can develop one's sense of the macabre.

As the months and years dragged on without the call, I began to suspect a conspiracy. I knew that Hillary's own nephrologist, Dr. Jerry Ruley, had qualms, at least in the abstract, about the principle of "wasting" precious organs in short supply on handicapped persons. I was ready to go to the mat with him or anyone else who took this position, for implicit in the thinking was the notion that handicapped people are less valuable than "normal" people. If Dr. Ruley had been evasive with me about his personal feelings on this point, he had assured me that in any event his personal feelings were no longer relevant. Hillary had been "listed"—that was the critical step—and once a person is listed, she becomes a number with merely a set of "values."

Perhaps. But year after year had passed without Hillary's getting the call. Had someone with a secret bias against the handicapped gone into the records and put an asterisk beside her name?

In tandem with this indefinite wait, our family started to receive a different kind of subtle pressure. Several nurses—never the doctors themselves—wondered if someone in our own family might be willing donate a kidney. The phrase here was "living donation." I could see why the doctors preferred this intrafamily gift. It made their life easier. The match of blood and tissue would be close, if not exact. The chances of rejection later would be lower. Almost everyone has an extra kidney, we were told breezily, which that person can easily do without, unless the person is a rugby player.

Denise leaped at the notion and rushed out to be tested. I watched her go wistfully, for I had told her that I was flatly opposed to her or our two "normal" children donating a kidney to Hillary and potentially jeopardizing their own health. I appreciated the noble instinct, but I would veto it. This led to some heated family spats. In her mind, Denise had been planning her own career moves— she was now a senior attorney at National Public Radio— around the time when Hillary's kidneys would finally fail completely, and she could then present her precious gift. She complained bitterly about my objections to me and to others, including Dr. Ruley.

"You're worried about just one person," Dr. Ruley replied. "He worries about two."

My objection stemmed from a conversation I'd had once with a Civil War historian, Dr. Gabor Boritt, during a long walk we took in the woods of Gettysburg in the early 1980s, just as Hillary's illness had become critical. We had talked about the impact of a desperate illness on the rest of the family, and Boritt warned me of how easily other family members could get sucked in and dragged down in situations like this. "Look out for the healthy ones," Gabor had said, and I remembered that. Hillary's illness was a given, and we would deal with it. But I was determined that the health of more Restons would not be compromised by it.

To Denise's dismay and my secret elation, her tests showed that her blood was now incompatible with Hillary's. The reasons were enough to make us weep, but for different reasons. During the early years of Hillary's illness, when she battled anemia along with everything else, Denise had given her own blood many times in a "directed donation," because she feared that AIDS had infected the general blood supply. The doctors had tried to reassure Denise, but she was adamant. In those days the implications of a mother donating blood to her child often were not understood. (My blood was of an entirely different type.) What an irony! Her noble act then had made a noble act now impossible. Hillary had developed antibodies to her own mother's blood.

Our only avenue, it seemed, was the "cadaveric" list.

[4]

Within her ever-expanding medical universe, Hillary was becoming quite a famous little girl. Doctors and nurses remembered her long after they had treated her. People who had known her as an infant asked after her a decade later. We took her back to see the doctor in New York, Dr. Stanley Resor Jr., who had first given us the bad news about mental retardation in 1983. He had seen many thousands of patients since, but he remembered Hillary. What did you expect nineteen years later? I asked him.

"I expected her to be a vegetable," he replied.

She had touched many hearts. In the second Kennedy Krieger hospitalization, her fame became national, but not exactly in a way we wanted.

During this second tour at Kennedy Krieger, a geneticist who was brought in to consult on Hillary's condition, Dr. Gerald Raymond, left Baltimore to attend a medical conference. There, by chance, he wandered into a session where the case of a rare, newly discovered genetic disorder was being presented. Its earmarks were nephrotic syndrome and immunological defect, but when Dr. Raymond heard that it also involved short stature, his ears perked up. They were describing Hillary, he thought.

Upon his return Dr. Raymond ordered T-cell tests for Hillary's immunological system and bone tests that might point to inherited traits. Though these tests were inconclusive, especially the ones dealing with her immune status, the burden of circumstantial evidence led to a firm conclusion: Hillary's overall afflication, explaining her entire clinical course from birth, was inherited, genetic in nature. He arranged for a meeting with Denise to present a formal diagnosis. Maureen van Stone, who now possessed the intimacy of family, was asked to attend. She knew what was coming.

In the flat clinical language of medical science, Dr. Raymond presented his finding. Hillary suffered a rare, hereditary, genetic disease that had been discovered in 1971 and only given a name in 1991. Less than a hundred people on the face of the Earth suffered from it. Its name was Schimke immuno-osseous dysplasia, or SID. With her intractable brain seizures and severe mental retardation, Hillary's condition added a new wrinkle to the syndrome, Dr. Raymond believed. Before her, there was no known case in the medical annals of SID being accompanied by brain seizures and severe mental retardation. She was therefore absolutely unique, from a medical point of view.

In awe and admiration, Maureen watched Denise receive this news with utter composure. At this totally unexpected, definitive conclusion Denise was clearly in shock and disbelief. Pointedly, she began with the ultimate question: Would Hillary die from the disease? No. The doctor did not think so. Would it change the course of her treatment? No. Would it alter Hillary's need for a kidney transplant? No. Indeed, SID patients had been transplanted before—although one had died after the transplant. Since Hillary had already been on the transplant waiting list for more than five years, would this be a further complication that might actually knock her off the list completely? Dr. Raymond did not see why.

And then he had a question of his own. Given this interesting new development for medical science, Dr. Raymond asked permission to write up Hillary's case for the *American Journal of Medical Genetics.* If Hillary's privacy could be protected, Denise was willing.

As the meeting was concluding, Hillary's mother had a final question.

"Could I have done anything differently?" she asked.

"It did not matter what you did," Dr. Raymond replied. The disease was going to assert itself with the brute force of inevitability. Hillary had been doomed from the beginning.

When Dr. Raymond disappeared down the hallway, Denise fell into Maureen's arms in sobs.

In the weeks afterward, I heard only hints of this shocking meeting. A theory for Hillary's overall condition had been put forward, and a name given to it. So what? It changed nothing: not her prognosis, not her treatment, not her need for a transplant. The process seemed to be driven by the need for order and neatness. I was skeptical. Once the fatalist in the family, the idea of the inevitability of a wicked, inherited seed appalled me. Of course, things could have been done along the way, maybe not by us, but by others. I was more comfortable with an explanation that had human hands all over it: high fevers that might have been moderated by a better doctor or by hospitalization; a stroke that was allowed negligently to happen, or whose severity and damage might have been tempered; overmedication leading to her kidney failure; and yes, fabulous doctoring at an intensive care unit that saved her life when she was supposed to die, and die early in life in this process of inevitability, like all the other kids who actually suffered from Schimke immuno-osseous dysplasia.

Denise listened to my objections and decided not to dwell on the point.

Dr. Raymond took on grotesque proportions in my mind. He was Dr. Death, or the proverbial cold scientist always looking, in the face of desperate illness, for neatness and order and immutable forces where there was only chaos and accident and human negligence. Perhaps he was one of those doctors out to protect other doctors.

I was not convinced.

CHAPTER TEN

[1]

As Hillary approached her eighteenth year to heaven, she stood at a stately four feet eight inches and weighed eighty pounds. If her brain had stalled somewhere close to the level of a two-year-old, her body appeared to be that of a ten-year-old. The only real benefit we could foresee was that for many years ahead our petite lady could still get into the movies for a child's price.

If she was short, she was perfectly proportioned. Her round, broad face and button nose, heart-shaped full mouth and lovely gray eyes imparted the look of a French mademoiselle. We loved to buy her all sorts of hats—in particular, straw hats with ribbons and bows that I cocked rakishly on a slant and spoke to her about in the few phrases of French I knew. She had sprouted little breasts, and legs that seemed long and fashionably willowy when you looked at them from a distance. She still walked with a jerky gait, feet pointed outward. It was a mannerism of which her doctors took note, for in kidney failure, one worried that her protein-starved bones would become brittle and honeycombed.

At last, our concern for her life waned. Dr. Conry had assured us that even in the bondage of dialysis Hillary could live to a ripe old age, so long as we were vigilant and attentive. We were so anyway; it had become second nature to us.

Consequently, we became increasingly preoccupied with her quality of life: Could she learn? How could she better communicate? How could we protect her from her own daredevil behavior? Was she receiving the right mix of medicines in her daily cocktail to minimize seizures, maximize her learning potential, and stave off other attacks to her fragile system? When was she at her happiest?

We had done our level best to nurture her happiness. In our eccentric storybook arts-and-crafts house, her second-floor room was her boudoir. It was shocking pink with gossamer silk drapes studded with little red hearts. We were laying it on a bit thick, I thought, and the room reminded me of Belle Watling's quarters in *Gone with the Wind*. On her bookshelves were a handful of Viennese music boxes and snow-filled globes, which she carried around the house with her as if they were her crystal balls. In her bathroom was an impressionistic poster with the caption, "Little girls with dreams become women with vision." On the windowsill was a slightly psychedelic fiber-and-light bouquet that somehow Denise had only been able to find in the Bronx. On the walls were posters of Audrey Hepburn and Claude Monet paintings from Giverny, along with my favorite, a poster I had brought back from Italy with the title *Immagini del Chianti*. It featured a powder-faced peasant girl with bunches of plump grapes for hair. When the lights went out at night, Hillary gazed dreamily at her grape stomper as if she were her awesome older sister. On the ceiling above her bed, we had stuck luminescent stars so that as she dropped off to sleep, she could contemplate the cosmos.

Music had also become important to her happiness. She was especially partial to Dame Joan Sutherland and Leontyne Price; the melodious, masculine tones of Pavarotti did nothing for her. The Indigo Girls and the Dixie Chicks were also high on her list, and on her door, we plastered bumper stickers with warnings like YIELD TO THE PRINCESS, GOD MADE ME A DANCING QUEEN, and CHICKS RULE. And how! Devin and I had had a tough time in this bawdy house. When we dressed her for school, the voice of Beth Nielsen Chapman boomed out "Happy Girl":

> *I didn't know until my soul broke free*
> *I've got these angels watching over me*
> *Oh watch me go.*
> *I'm the happy girl . . .*

At nighttime we often put her to sleep with the strains of *Wind & Mountain* mood music that we had picked up at a sensuous hot spring outside Santa Fe.

It had been years since we had thought of her as retarded. We had entered Phase III, where the embarrassments and the surprises were few, and Hillary had become merely an interesting and quite well-known figure in the community. Store owners acknowledged her affectionately and spoke to her frequently, knowing full well that while she might not understand the words, she would appreciate the sentiment.

We did not define her as handicapped, nor did she define herself so. A life force surged within her; it was only dampened when she was sick or sedated or overmedicated, which was often. Parts of her brain worked very well indeed. She could be devilish and manipulative. She knew how to amuse us, and how to amuse herself. She knew how to work her will, sometimes with such single-mindedness that we would call her a tyrant or a Nazi. Her demands had to come first—a trait we only later understood to be a real sore spot in the upbringing of her siblings, Maeve and Devin, who in our never-ending crises had to come second. We could sometimes forget that Dr. Boritt's shibboleth, "Look out for the healthy ones," meant take care of them not only physically, but emotionally as well.

Hillary had developed a habit of sitting demurely on her legs as if she were a geisha in a teahouse. When she sat that way at the beach, watching the waves crash on the shore, or before a fire, watching the glowing embers, we knew she was contemplating the eternal verities. She had also developed a hilarious set of gestures. Dull-witted doctors called these "stereotyped gestures," but that sucked all the fun out of them. One of her frequent habits was to throw her arm straight out and then open her thumb and index finger, as if she were tossing a seed over a fence. This reminded us of John Travolta in *Saturday Night Fever,* and we were given to bursting into the strains of "Stayin' Alive" when she did it.

Her spatial awareness was extraordinary. It manifested itself in being able to solve the most intricate of puzzles, often far faster than her peers with their "normal" brains. These "normal" kids solved their puzzles by consulting the overall design on the box; Hillary worked solely by the shape of the individual pieces. She also had a keen memory. Everything in her personal space had to be just so. When it was not, she would throw her arm straight out at the out-of-place item and squeal a demand for order.

Her religious preference was decidedly druid, for she had an intimate if slightly adversarial relationship with nature. At low branches of trees or bushes, she would tarry and swat the outliers, as if they were the advance guard of some hostile force. When she arrived home from school, she took real pleasure in kicking the mums that festooned our outside stairway. At Fiery Run no joy was greater than to sit by the stream for hours and throw sticks into the slow-moving water. As I watched this from a distance on a sparkling day, I longed to be Andrew Wyeth.

Whatever the world might think—that Hillary was subhuman or of lesser value, a ward of the state or a drag on society—she dominated her world in her full humanness and rich personhood. She had taken possession of our lives. She was a social, convivial person who loved people and crowds. (She had been born in New York, after all.) The roar of the crowd and the crack of the bat were in her blood and genes. Over the years we took her to Macy's parades and window gazings along Fifth Avenue at Christmastime and baseball games galore. At Memorial Stadium in Baltimore or Shea Stadium in New York, no one seemed to mind her squeals of delight or even her penchant for lobbing M&M's into the seats below us. Wherever there was a throng, Hillary was in her element.

In these intervening years, we had come to our separate resolutions. Mine was more of a peace, a quiet resignation. We—and Hillary most of all—had been dealt a very bad hand, something like the dark reverse of a straight flush in poker, except in our case the deck had many more than fifty-two cards and the chances of drawing this profoundly losing hand were minuscule. Perhaps a better image is "winning" a diabolical lottery in which the chances of your number coming up is something like 200 in 6 billion.

As the fatalist of the family, I was devoted to Hillary's care, and it gave me great satisfaction. The joys of having a Perpetual Child in the house had begun to dawn on me. Hillary kept me on my toes. She kept us connected and vital. I was approaching my sixtieth year, and people remarked on how young I looked for my age as I trundled off to a national tennis championship in Tucson, Arizona.

I had happily dispensed with the frills of life and asked only to raise my children and write my books. I wrote four in those twelve years, and the research for them took me far away: to the dusty byways of rural Texas for politics as a raw American art form, to the baseball parks of the American pastime and the ivory towers of academe, to exotic, foreign venues where Galileo had turned his telescope to the sky and had been tried for heresy.

These forays were all interesting and productive, but I enjoyed their pleasures emptily. I had tired of traveling, for it could be nerve-racking. Once when I was in Berlin, Denise called with the latest Hillary emergency, and there was, of course, nothing I could do about it but fret. Later, when I was even farther away, in Iran, every day became torture. What would I do if . . . ? To be gone for more than two weeks made me feel guilty.

If my Phase III was the stage of serene acceptance, it was dogged by the ever-present question of what had happened to my child. I was committed to finding an answer. I began to pay more attention to the increasing number of articles in the paper about genetic medicine and the human genome. Could it be that we would find an answer to our family fate in this brave new world?

Denise remained in a perpetual state of war. Her Catholicism and her motherhood and her hot-tempered street sense made her angrier, more frustrated, and more despairing, just as she was more passionate in refusing to accept the status quo. To her, being fatalistic meant giving up, surrendering to the blandishments and the obfuscations of doctors. This unrelenting war was wearing her out, I could tell, and its strains were heaped on top of her major work responsibilities. She was buying buildings, protecting reporters from lawsuits, and negotiating contracts and licenses for that national treasure known as National Public Radio. Juggling the strains of Hillary's care and her duties as an executive of a major news organization was a challenge no man I know could handle. There were times when her worry made her look older than her years. She was not ready to give up the search to find, if not a cure or a miracle, then at least some avenue to better Hillary's quality of life. Neither of us could accept this "no-name disease" that had destroyed two major organs in our child's body.

Meanwhile, our elder children were growing up. Maeve had developed into a tart-tongued sophomore at Cornell; she remarked that our care of Hillary was our preparation for sainthood. We laughed. At last we could feel her sense of liberation. We appreciated the unfair, colossal burden that is placed on all siblings of handicapped children.

Over the years Maeve and Devin had dealt with this burden in profoundly different ways. Quite naturally, little girls feel the embarrassment in public more keenly, and Maeve was no exception. She had come to dread our trips out into the world, for she never knew how they would go. When Hillary was bad, with screams that seemed almost inhuman at times, or if she launched her dinnertime missiles, Maeve felt like crawling under the table. She was furious at her sister and wanted to shake her into behaving, only to become overcome with guilt for the impulse. Intellectually, she knew her little sister was not doing this on purpose. If someone looked at her train wreck of a family the wrong way, Maeve was afraid her mother would jump down the stranger's throat with some withering remark. Why couldn't she be part of a family that just went out and had a good time? Why must every outing be a drama? When year after year the family trundled off for yet another Disney World vacation, Maeve tired of the permanent child at the heart of the family and sought escape.

As she grew into a popular teenager, Maeve, by her own admission, became a control freak and a perfectionist. Everything around her had to be just so. She hated to be criticized, she hated disorder, and she hated conflict. If there was conflict, it needed to be resolved immediately. To some she came off as prim and proper to the point of being prissy. To her parents, she often seemed oblivious to her little sister, and only later did we come to understand that we were confusing perfectly normal adolescent behavior for indifference or insensitivity. When Denise would suggest that Maeve take Hillary out once in a while with her friends, saying such things as "Well, Hillary will never get a chance to go to a prom," Maeve recoiled in horror. At age fifteen she was not entirely sure she was going to feel comfortable at a high-school party alone, much less with her strange sister in tow.

When she finally went off to college, we could feel her burden being lifted, and we rejoiced for her. But there was a residue: She had become an exceedingly compassionate, empathetic, and responsible person, while at the same time she had turned inward. A view of life was taking shape: Her world could be just fine, and then fall apart in a second for no good reason. She could not count on even the most normal things working out, for life was unfair, and the possibilities of getting blindsided were great. This view of the world as a precarious place would come to affect her relationships later with her friends and her employers. When she went to work at a newspaper in her early twenties, she lived in terror that a single mistake would result not only in her firing, but in being driven from the profession forever. She was drawn to medical students for boyfriends.

Devin, in turn, suffered from different inner demons. Why had Hillary been struck down and not him? What did she do to deserve this, rather than him? She was smart. He knew her to be a wonderful person. He had seen her in the ICU, so weak and yet so strong in fighting for her life, and his admiration soared. He thought to himself that her strength of character was so much greater than his own. His first memory as a child of five was the vision of Hillary on the brink of death. He remembered Dr. Peebles's red mustache and his incandescent lecture— Hillary was very, very sick, and she might go away for a long sleep—and our demand: that he must now say good-bye. It was not until Devin became a teenager himself that we all came to a stark realization. At age five, Devin had developed a case of post-traumatic stress disorder.

As Maeve sought to distance herself from the horror, Devin embraced it. He was alternately angry and tender with Hillary—angry because she was stealing so much of his parents' attention, tender because she needed his help. He announced his desire to be a brain surgeon or a pediatrician when he grew up; these bespoke Devin's "major rescue fantasies," his doctor told us. In countless ways he tried to make Hillary normal—or if he could not make her normal like him, he sought to be abnormal like her. He made a point of bringing his friends home to introduce them to Hillary. Just because she had had a stroke, he thought, it didn't mean she didn't like boys. Let them come so she could make eyes at them. He never felt embarrassment with her in public. In his mind, he had become her "interpreter" to the world, for he, better than any of us, could decipher her coded, encrypted language and could convey to others what she was feeling and thinking.

"I am her voice," he said.

From this hidden survivor's guilt, from this determination to join her at the same level (wherever that might be), Devin's performance in grade school suffered. His parents and his teachers were mystified at why so bright a student could excel for half a term, and then suddenly crash in lethargy and disinterest. His modest grades, especially in the sciences like biology, were destroying one of his fondest childhood dreams: that one day he would become a brilliant neurologist who would discover the cure that would enable Hillary to speak again. Only years later did we understand that academic shortcomings were Devin's message to Hillary. They were in this together. They were a team.

But the real flashpoint between father and son came over the issue of a transplant. When it became clear that Denise could not donate, Devin stepped forward. In our family, only he now was compatible with Hillary's blood and tissue type. He wanted to be tested. To his disappointment and lasting anger, I flatly vetoed it. I had already lost half a daughter, I told him. I would not countenance losing half a son as well. Protect the healthy ones. That had become my mantra. Devin never quite forgave me. In desperation, he turned to his mother. Between them they made a secret pact: If Hillary began to dwindle to a critical point, Denise would come to me and persuade me to rescind my objection.

Meanwhile, appreciating the strength of his bond to Hillary, we did our best to minimize his duties, but even so they were considerable. As far as we were concerned, the sooner he, too, was liberated the better. We worried that when liberation came it might be too late.

As he went off to college on the West Coast in 1998, he wrote a poem.

> *Imagine a world of laughter and joy.*
> *Of soft pastel sunsets when the sky is all on fire.*

The year I was four and played in the fields where
   the grass was golden.
So was my spirit.
She got sick that winter.
We watched the flakes fall—the sands in an
   hourglass.
By that summer she had spoke her last.
She uttered sounds but no words would come.
This was prologue to my life to date:
One of doctors and hospitals for her and pain for
   me.
The sun is not above me in the heavens.
As I move west, it's in my eyes.
No other nineteen-year-old will have to give a
   kidney at thirty-one.
I want to live every day as my last.
I know the light will fade—night will come maybe
   at thirty-one.
My moods are a blessing and a curse—
A ride like no other and a hurt like no other.
Maybe I will live until one hundred and ten.
But I fear she won't be so lucky.
I can't think of that now—I'll think about that
   tomorrow—but I fear and I hope.
Not a soul can imagine what it's like—
I love my sister more than myself.
I often wonder why I didn't have the stroke?
Could I handle such an illness?
She is so brave—so sweet—so good.

What am I? Will I know
When the purple and orange alpine glow is on the
  mountains?

Will I be satisfied?
Will she paint the sunsets?

[2]

For Hillary's eighteenth birthday, we decided to have a real blowout. All of her doctors and caregivers, teachers and admirers—of which there were many over the years—were invited. An immense cake was ordered, the house draped with the kudzu of crepe paper. Of course, there were balloons, scores of them in every room. Hillary and balloons go together.

When we wrote out the guest list, we realized how she had become a major presence in the lives of so many. Even the regrets, like that of Dr. Conry, who had to be away at a professional conference in Florida, possessed a special wistfulness. One note, from her school nurse, Robin Peters, read: "It is always a joy to work with Hillary. She is very strong, and she has an innate dignity which is very appealing and inspiring." "An innate dignity" . . . yes, it was true.

For her bash we chose a deep-green velvet, long-sleeved moiré taffeta ensemble, cinched in the middle with a black belt and puffed into a full skirt with crinoline petticoats. We coiffed her hair, carefully placed a black bow on one side, and finished off the look with black patent-leather pumps. When the hour came, we arranged her glamorously on our large L-shaped living-room couch and waited for the first knock on the door. Of the many unique aspects of Hillary's life, she had no sense of anticipation. But she knew something special was up. The dress alone told the story.

As they came through the door one by one—the doctors and nurses who had saved her life, the psychologists and behavior modification experts who had imparted to her human condition some measure of control, the teachers who had sought to maximize her potential, the caregivers who had lavished their love and energy on her—Hillary seemed as if she would jump out of her skin. One, such as Helen Weisel, would have been enough to catapult her into the outer reaches of joy, but this was the whole cast. She shouted her jubilation to the neighborhood at first, but as her mentors kept coming and coming until our living room had standing room only, and as they vied for a seat closer to her, on the couch or the floor, in some sort of pecking order, she quieted down, and an expression of awe came over her face. She looked from one to another and another, all of them people with whom she had had such intense, intimate relationships over the years; you could see her mind processing the memories. With her eyes and her sounds, she was saying, "You remember the time when . . ." Some things are better left unsaid.

We, too, were in awe.

CHAPTER ELEVEN

---

[1]

In the summer of 1999, I received an irresistible invitation from an old friend, Dr. Cosimo Mazzoni, to attend an international conference in Florence, Italy. Cosimo is a professor of law at the University of Siena who happens also to be an Italian count and squire of an elegant villa called Montececeri, located high above Florence in Fiesole. During pleasant times in the past, when I was working on my Galileo biography in the early 1990s, I stood with Cosimo on an outcropping of rock on his property where Leonardo da Vinci tested one of his flying machines in the fifteenth century, no doubt with slaves. (Only later did I learn that many high rock outcroppings in Italy claim this dubious distinction.) Cosimo and his hilarious, gorgeous, freckle-faced wife, Antonella Berardi, who is a well-known set designer for Italian opera and film, had been kind and nurturing to a writer in need, and we had become close.

Cosimo's conference was on the subject of cloning. Its purpose was to bring together a diverse group of geneticists, jurists, philosophers, and writers to discuss the legal, social, and philosophical implications of the first cloned human being, which seemed to be an event in the offing. The last day of the conference, for which Cosimo especially wanted me present, was to consider the topic cloning and the popular imagination. The session was to be chaired by Umberto Eco.

The ethical storm over the possibility of artificially reproducing an exact copy of an existing human being in a laboratory was already well under way. With the birth of Dolly the sheep—an event that shook the world—and the subsequent cloning of pigs, mice, cats, rabbits, and cows, the technology for adapting the techniques to human beings seemed to be at hand. If the birth of a modern Frankenstein was abhorrent to most, the process along the way—specifically, the production of stem cells from human embryos—held out the potential for great advances in medicine. With stem cells, the medical profession argued, all manner of common and rare diseases could be cured. Diabetes and Parkinson's disease were usually mentioned in the news articles. What about Schimke immuno-osseous dysplasia? I wondered.

By the time of my Florence trip, sentiment in Congress was moving toward banning human cloning altogether—the Human Cloning Prohibition Act was passed in 2001—but the law would only bar the use of federal monies in cloning research and experimentation. President Bill Clinton had supported the ban on cloning and stem-cell research (but two years later, his successor, George W. Bush, opened the door a crack by permitting the first highly limited foray into the field with federal blessing). Meanwhile, a high-ranking British science and ethics commission recommended that researchers there be allowed to create cloned human embryos for some research purposes, so long as the embryos were destroyed within fourteen days. And inevitably, Pope John Paul II waded in by praising the world's medical community for its development of organ transplants, but condemned the cloning of human embryos to produce organs as "morally unacceptable, even when its proposed goal is good in itself."

Thus, we were hearing a great deal from the scientist's or physician's or politician's or spiritual leader's or abortion protester's point of view, but nothing from the standpoint of the consumer or the client for this breathtaking new research. I was taking it all very personally.

As I prepared to travel abroad, a number of articles had been appearing in the American press about events that seemed relevant to the conference. An article in the *New York Times* carried the headline "Human-Cow Hybrid Cells Are Topic of Ethics Panel." Deep in the article, one of a myriad about stem-cell research that were to usher from our papers in the coming years, was this paragraph: "The hybrid cow-human cells consist of the nucleus of a human cell inserted into a cow egg whose own nucleus has been removed. Factors in the cow egg are thought to make the human cell nucleus revert to its embryonic form." To this nonscientist, it seemed as if medical science was on the road to producing Minotaurs in the new millennium.

The week before my departure, front pages blared the news of the tragic death of Jesse Gelsinger, the eighteen-year-old from Philadelphia who suffered from a rare genetic disorder and had volunteered for experimental gene therapy. The Gelsinger scandal would widen that fall when it emerged that more than a dozen other volunteers for gene therapy had been inadvertently infected with the AIDS virus. The scandal grew wider still when Gelsinger's father testified before Congress that his son's Philadelphia doctors had misled the family about the risks involved in the experiment.

I read these stories with rapt attention, for they all seemed relevant to Hillary. My heart went out to Gelsinger's parents, for we knew only too well the ambivalence of parents to whom new, experimental therapies are proposed when old therapies prove inadequate. Dr. Conry's line from years before reverberated in our heads: "We can always give your child another poison."

But her remark had emerged from the old way of doing things. Now we were on the cusp of the new age of genetic medicine. Science fiction and Hollywood movies like *Gattaca* had speculated what this new age would be like. Twenty years from now, we imagined, someone would draw a drop of Hillary's blood, or scrape her delicate skin, enter the information into a computer, and shazam! We would find the exact mutation of the specific gene on a particular line of genes in the suspect gene field. Only with such genetic tools could we nail the diagnosis.

With such magic, would it turn out that she indeed had Schimke immuno-osseous dysplasia? Once they identified the mutation, would they go in for the repair—for what good was diagnosis without cure? This would be the so-called somatic cell gene therapy, where the defective part was replaced, either from human material developed from stem cells or from animal cells, as if it were a spent spark plug. And perhaps they wouldn't stop there. Then they would cadge samples from our other two children and determine if they were carriers of the defect. If they were, the wizards would go forward with "germ-line gene intervention," modifying our children's imperfect genetic endowment.

The old methods had all been tried on Hillary. She remained a puzzling mystery. Our visits to doctors' offices took on a certain dull sameness. Her doctors had become mere caretakers. We began to detect a hint of annoyance when we called with familiar crises in the middle of the night. They seemed to have become bored with her case.

We needed new energy, new approaches, fresh faces, new ideas. We longed for someone on the cutting edge, perhaps in this new area of genetic medicine, to take an interest in her. Like the parents of Jesse Gelsinger, we were quite ready to offer Hillary up as an experimental laboratory animal, if only some medical sleuth might offer hope for an improvement in her quality of life. Denise even harbored the dream that perhaps brain cells from some source, even if it were a nonhuman source, might be injected into the dead spaces and stagnant pools of Hillary's brain, and suddenly she would talk again. If the cells were animal, I dreamed that she would wake up snorting like a pig.

And so I was going to Florence not only as a writer who had long tried to engage popular imagination on a host of subjects, but as a potential client for these world-class geneticists and their new medicine. We were the future recipients or, to put it in commercial terms, future consumers of the new wisdom.

In the week before I left for Florence, I asked Hillary's kidney doctor, Dr. Jerry Ruley, whether medical research held out any hope for growing a kidney in the laboratory. For the reality we faced if Hillary were ever to get a kidney transplant haunted me. Our gain would be someone else's catastrophe. Hillary could only get a cadaveric kidney from a human corpse, probably a youthful corpse at that. And so, in the five years on the kidney transplant list, we were, in effect, waiting for a truck to hit someone else's child, and hoping that tragedy would produce an organ that matched Hillary's blood type and antigens. In my discussions with the transplant doctors, I shrank from ever asking where the organs came from.

The flatness of transplant language interested me. It possessed a dull, dehumanized quality the purpose of which was to cover up the ghoulish situation that both the donor and the recipient face. We had to wait for just the right organ with just the right numbers to become available, and then hope that the "harvesting" was skillful. Doctors often said to us that getting the right kidney off the list was "a crapshoot." Some craps game.

In answer to my question about impending breakthroughs in the laboratory, Ruley answered that no, a kidney was not likely to be manufactured from stem cells in a lab. Stupid though the organ's function might be, the architecture of a kidney is complicated. That was the brilliance of nature. A kidney involves too many cells with different functions ever to be "grown" artificially.

We should rest our hopes, he suggested, in xenografts . . . or in human clones.

A xenograft, I quickly learned, is a pig organ that has been "immunologically stripped" of its pigness, so that the human body will not reject this donation from another species. In its infinite sense of humor, the medical profession had dubbed these genetically modified creatures "nude pigs." They were also known as transgenic pigs. The first transgenic pigs were born in Blacksburg, Virginia, in March 2002, as if to usher in the biology of the new millennium. These first transgenic pigs were also cloned pigs, in which a "foreign marker gene" had been introduced into their DNA structure.

The same company that gave us the first cloned sheep,

Dolly, two years earlier, had orchestrated these births. In the euphoric press release about the event, the company, PPL Therapeutics, trumpeted the possibility that clinical trials could begin within five years, and a $5 billion industry for solid organs alone would follow. We could imagine animal farms all over America with shameless nude pigs ready to fuel this new billion-dollar industry with their neutralized, species-less body parts. It promised a Huxleyan brave new world where in every hospital an Organ Store did a brisk business in the subbasement when the needy came to shop for an off-the-shelf spare part.

This was, I suppose, good news for Hillary.

The problem with this wizardry was twofold. Nature still had a few surprises up its sleeve. A xenograft, for all its immunological stripping, could, when transplanted into a human, create a retrovirus, a disease unknown to mankind and therefore impossible to treat. Thus, the recipient might be responsible for spreading a terrible epidemic around the world. The second problem was philosophical. If xenografts were successful, Dr. Ruley said, it was the end of evolution by natural selection. It presaged the end of *Homo sapiens* (translated as wise man), and the beginning of *Homo suillus* (pig man).

[2]

In the tawny hills above Florence, at the Instituto Universitario Europeo de San Domenico in Fiesole, we gathered around a large rectangular table as if this were the United

Nations Security Council. The translators hovered behind glass, and I donned my headphones in grand diplomatic fashion. In their various tongues, the geneticists reported on the progress of the human genome map. A French sociologist, Dominique Mehl, spoke of the shock in her Catholic country over the birth of Dolly. One doctor, Carlo Falmigni, the president of the Italian Society for Fertility and Sterility, in arguing against any restriction whatever on cloning research, asserted that no government had a moral right to restrict the advancement of knowledge. All knowledge was by its nature moral, he proclaimed. Another expert compared the efforts to restrict cloning as equivalent to the Vatican's restrictions on Galileo's astronomy in 1616. Legal scholars addressed the international laws against cloning and the ways that they would surely be circumvented.

But the lightning rod of the conference was Dr. John Finnis, a firebrand of an Oxford philosopher and a Catholic who was a chief adviser to Pope John Paul II on the ethics of biotechnology. Only Finnis used the word *evil*, when he addressed the whole gamut of biological manipulations that would lead, he said breezily, to the first human clone in the coming two years, and to the general worldwide acceptance of human cloning within ten years. These clones would be the new slaves or worse, the new providers of pulsating meat products for human consumption. Perhaps, it had been suggested, these clones could be born without brains, and hence, they would be known as "headless clones."

Focusing on Louise Brown, the first human being to

be conceived in an incubator in the process known as in vitro fertilization, Finnis spoke of the change in attitude toward Dr. Robert Edwards, the British doctor who had hatched her. For years, Dr. Edwards had been reviled and ostracized within his profession for his work. But after the decanting of Louise Brown, these same colleagues rose en masse to applaud him.

"We should recognize," Finnis said, "that the crowd, including the crowd of the learned, will follow power and technical opportunity. But we don't have to applaud."

The same attitude, he implied, would take place when the world was shaken by the birth of the first human clone. We were fast on the road to Huxley's Central London Hatchery and Conditioning Center. We were going to get it all, he told me later, and very soon.

These were heady thoughts, and I pondered them in my brocaded hotel room on the banks of the Arno as I prepared my paper, which was entitled "Nude Pigs and Headless Clones." To my disappointment, Umberto Eco did not show up on the third day of the conference. As consolation Cosimo asked me to chair the day's proceedings in Eco's absence. There was much talk of Aldous Huxley and Frankenstein, and about how, in science's negligence in policing itself on cloning, future horrors would be defined by filmmakers and writers rather than scientists. In my presentation I quoted Huxley's foreword to the 1946 edition of *Brave New World:* "A book about the future can only interest us if its prophecies look as if they might conceivably come true."

When the lively proceedings were over, we repaired to a medieval club near the Medici Palace for champagne and dinner. There, over drinks, I fell into conversation with a world-renowned Italian geneticist, Alberto Piazza, who had coauthored a seminal work on population genetics called *The History and Geography of Human Genes.* I told him that I was thinking about doing this book about Hillary.

"Don't do it," he counseled. "It will upset your healthy children."

CHAPTER TWELVE

---

[1]

For years, it seemed, I had been traveling with Hillary. Most of these voyages were in my head and in my dreams, but some were real. Two memorable ones took place in 2001. In February of that year we went to Salt Lake City to visit old friends and to ski at Alta. Hillary went with us, and even took several ski lessons in the "adaptive" program. She made a lovely picture under the brilliant sunshine as she slid down a gradual slope, eyes lifted stoically to the peaks, gentle as you please, as if her mind were a thousand miles away. After my spectacular wipeouts, I envied her lack of anxiety.

The trip was also an opportunity to have a talk with

Dr. Mario Capecchi. I had been given an introduction to this world-famous genetic engineer and was told that he was a leading candidate for the next Nobel Prize. Denise and I felt a bit embarrassed for taking up the valuable time of so distinguished a scientist for our little introduction to Genetics 101. But we blundered forward anyway in the certain knowledge that dumb-boy tactics in the past had paid great dividends.

While the nature of Dr. Capecchi's research was far beyond my understanding, I thought of him as a master manipulator of mice and almost expected him to wear some sort of a costume, like a lion tamer in a small circus. Since, as the experts assure us, mice and humans are close evolutionary relatives, he had conducted a number of seminal studies on the operation of specific genes in mice that might be similar in humans, including one well-publicized study identifying the grooming gene. (Mice, the study showed, could be just as obsessive-compulsive about their looks as my elder daughter.) In 2001 he was working on splicing embryonic stem cells into cloned mice, manipulating their DNA, and replacing faulty genes with healthy ones from the clone in a process known as "homologous recombination." Homologous recombination was relevant to the repair of defective genes, in the genetic medicine of the future, and so theoretically seemed relevant to Hillary—or at least to the Hillary of twenty years hence.

As usual this work led to wonderful terminology. Dr. Capecchi had created a "knockout mouse," meaning a mouse with a certain undesirable gene silenced. All I could think of was the favorite cartoon figure of my wispy, underweight youth, Mighty Mouse, but his genes were scarcely silenced.

One snowy morning we bundled Hillary up and went to the Eccles Institute of Human Genetics at the University of Utah, a sparkling new facility of glass and aluminum. We climbed the staircase of its atrium, designed to suggest the double helix of DNA, and stood outside Dr. Capecchi's lab, staring at a bewildering poster that covered a huge space and contained the rough draft of the human genome map. Somewhere in those smudges of short and long lines, I thought, lies Hillary's problem. We felt a certain sense of trepidation. This was to be the first time that Denise and I went together to an expert to discuss the possibility of a genetic disorder in Hillary.

We were ushered into the presence of a muscular, middle-aged man with disheveled hair and a quiet manner, dressed for the weather in boots and a flannel shirt. Dr. Capecchi was welcoming and put us immediately at ease. As Hillary curled up in a swivel chair and went to sleep, Dr. Capecchi came right to the point. We were under a misapprehension, he said, if we thought that the genome map could confirm or deny Hillary's diagnosis anytime soon. Nor were we anywhere near the time when her condition might be repaired with gene therapy. It was not, as we thought, a simple matter, just like in the movies, of drawing a drop of blood, matching its numbers and letters to a computer database, and nailing the problem. While the field was moving very quickly, it was moving unevenly, with most of the attention focused on widespread diseases like schizophrenia or Alzheimer's disease that were known to be genetic.

We had to hope for a doctor somewhere who was interested in a disease that plagued fewer than a hundred people on the face of the Earth. If this oddball existed, then we should join his group. The more "robust" the "pedigree," Capecchi said, the better the chance of identifying its genetic information, of isolating the specific DNA. But such a study would be for the benefit not of Hillary but of future Schimke sufferers.

If there were a doctor somewhere who was focused on Schimke and who had a robust group of sufferers, it would probably be ten years before he could identify the specific mutation. When Dr. Capecchi mentioned our Hillary as a possible heterozygote, with different alleles (variant forms of the same gene) at the same locus, or, worse, as a possible homozygote (the product of like pairs of faulty genes from each parent), I knew we had entered the brave new world.

Our first and largest step, Dr. Capecchi said, was to determine whether in fact Hillary's illness was genetic. If it was not genetic, the chance she had had in the womb of developing her disease was 1 in 100,000. If it was genetic, her chance had been 1 in 3 billion. The shock of these numbers numbed us. As if to comfort us, Capecchi pointed out that all humans had at least a hundred to perhaps a thousand mutations in their genetic makeup. No one is perfect, he said.

"You mean, we are all a bundle of errors and omissions?" Denise piped up, ever the consummate lawyer. ("Errors and omissions" is a catchphrase of insurance law, and here it was being applied to an imaginary contract between mankind and its Maker.)

The remark was more than witty. Between my concept of a bad seed and Denise's concept of human beings as less than perfect lay a difference in religious outlook. The notion of a bad seed comes from my latent Calvinist upbringing, in which I was taught that God eternally punishes man for original sin and elects to heaven only those whose good deeds far outweigh their bad. Denise's Catholic God conferred forgiveness and redemption on his imperfect flock.

[2]

In May 2001 Hillary was accepted at the National Institutes of Health (NIH) under a new research protocol. Her acceptance was a recognition of her uniqueness . . . and her worthiness as a research subject. Perhaps she was a unique creature on the face of the earth; I derived some pleasure from that thought. Part of her uniqueness, of course, lay in the fact that she had survived so many disasters. Our daughter, the escape artist. If she really had Schimke immuno-osseous dysplasia, she should have been dead at the age of four. She nearly was, I had to remind myself.

This protocol of one would be managed by a geneticist, Dr. Donna Krasnewich, who was the clinical director of the genetics service at the NIH hospital. A straight-talking, bighearted Midwesterner who apologized jokingly for never helping out her patients by anglicizing her Polish name, Dr. Krasnewich promised to work with me both to try to arrive at a solid diagnosis for Hillary's overall condition and to advocate for her on the transplant front.

At last we had found a doctor on the cutting edge of the new medicine who would bring the new energy we longed for. Her interest in Hillary and in our family was genuine and manifest. As it happened, Dr. Krasnewich's empathy stemmed partly from a personal source. I should have known: She, too, had a child with neurological difficulties. This was becoming a pattern. Dr. K was the third of Hillary's doctors who in their personal lives had experienced their own tragedies. Ten years before, Hillary's deeply caring neurologist, Dr. Joan Conry, had lost her third child, also a daughter, to a rare bone-marrow disease. And only two years earlier, Hillary's primary kidney doctor, Dr. Glenn Bock, had learned that his son suffered from Tourette's syndrome. "It makes me a better doctor," Dr. Bock had told me.

For the next six months, in wide reading and in various talks with Dr. K and others at NIH, I tried to build up my knowledge of genetics. What was the relationship of cells to chromosomes? Of chromosomes to DNA? Of DNA to genes? Of dominant and recessive genes? Of recessive genes to their mutations? Of mutations to disease?

The numbers were sometimes daunting, sometimes comprehensible. The first draft of the human genome, which had only been published early in 2001, put the number of genes in the human endowment at thirty-two thousand, of which a few thousand so far correlated to disease. That seemed manageable enough. But then to identify a specific gene or a suspect area, much less its mutation, the doctor had to examine a patient's DNA, and for DNA there were 3 billion base pairs, and millions of variants. There was more to this than merely taking a drop of blood and matching its numbers in a computer.

I could only understand our predicament, I concluded, if I kept a laser beam on Hillary's case alone.

Then there was the political side. With only a "rough sketch" of the human genome in hand, the world of medicine would naturally focus first on the genes that implicated the most common diseases like Parkinson's, cystic fibrosis, and Alzheimer's. Medicine had to have its priorities. Focus on rare diseases would come later, as Dr. Capecchi had said, since with rare disorders there was a "small research base," and no product development. Follow the money. The fortunes for companies and individuals lay in new product development for common diseases; rare diseases were "orphaned." And so, we were told, as a threadbare orphan we would probably have to wait five to ten years until the rough draft of the map was polished, and some minor-league doctor became interested in a little German off in the shadows called Schimke.

In her efforts to make me understand, Dr. Krasnewich appealed to my literary side. She invited me to think of Hillary as a writer like myself.

"Hillary is now old enough to write her own book,"

she said. "She has been on a stable course for sixteen years. No matter what label we put on her, Schimke or something else, it will not affect her prognosis, or how we care for her. She should live a long, long time."

And then we got into the details. The DNA of every gene in the humane genome is comprised of four base letters, T, C, A, and G, and these DNA letters are different for each gene. A disorder comes from a misspelling within the gene—a C where a T should be, for example. Thus, to find the genetic explanation for Schimke the researcher had to (1) find the candidate area or band, (2) identify the gene itself, and (3) find the misspelling (or mutation) within the gene's DNA that is common to all Schimke sufferers.

If Hillary had the disease, it probably came from a recessive gene, the small r gene that did not express itself normally. "And probably harbored resentment as a result," I thought, "ready to reap revenge." In other words, Denise and I, while unaffected ourselves, were carriers of the same misspelled gene. That had been our incredible misfortune. It was as if Denise were the *Encyclopedia Americana* and I was the *Encyclopaedia Britannica,* and when we got together, we found we had misspelled the same sentence in the same entry in the fifteenth volume.

"Look at it this way," Dr. K said. "Let's say the normal sentence for the gene where Schimke can reside reads: 'The cat jumped over the moon.' With that sentence a person is fine. Each person gets two copies of every gene, one from the mom, one from the dad. For their child to get Schimke, the mom and the dad would have to donate the same misspelled sentence, say, 'The bat jumped over the moon.'"

"And what are the chances of that happening?" I asked.

"About one in a hundred thousand," she answered.

For its cures this new genetic medicine would act like a giant spell-checker. Forty years from now all Americans would wear a biochip around their neck in which their entire genetic endowment would be stored. In an emergency the chip would tell the tale immediately, and tell the doctor what to do. For the Hillarys of the future, the computer would highlight the DNA's misspelling in a single gene, and then with a tap of a key correct the misspelling.

"Is this the way it will work?" I asked Dr. Krasnewich. I imagined a baby's genetics being changed in the delivery room.

"That's too late," she replied. "The current technology is already there to identify a disorder . . ."

"In utero?" I interjected.

"No, in the sperm and in the egg. Even before conception it's possible to mutate an abnormality back to what it's supposed to be. The question is, should this technology be used? How far should genetic screening go?"

"What is the outer limit?" I asked.

"If, for example, you know from the sperm that a child will have a birthmark, should you correct it? If you prefer coarse to fine hair, should you be able to choose? With genetic manipulation, where do you stop?"

"What are the implications of this for a Hillary forty years from now?" I asked.

"That a child like Hillary would not be born," she answered.

[3]

In mid-2001 a computer search at NIH turned up the name of a Houston doctor who was focused on Schimke immuno-osseus dysplasia. Dr. Cornelius Boerkoel, at the Baylor College of Medicine, had written a number of articles about Schimke. (We noticed that several had been referenced in the article about Hillary by the Johns Hopkins doctor two years earlier.) Moreover, Dr. Boerkoel was conducting a study of Schimke in an active search for the suspect gene, and was actively recruiting patients who were said to have the condition.

And so we had our expert. This was the kind of study Dr. Capecchi in Salt Lake City had hoped (against hope) might surface. Even if it would only help the sufferers of the future, even if it might take ten years before the dot on the human genome map could be pinpointed, Capecchi had said, we should do it.

In December we decided to visit our elder daughter, Maeve, who was completing her second year at an Austin, Texas, newspaper. This was the moment to take Hillary to the doctor who knew more about her supposed disease than anyone on the planet.

And so I called him up.

"I fully understand that it may be ten years before you complete your study and can tell us whether Hillary has the disease . . . ," I began.

"It won't take ten years," said the husky voice on the line. "I have cloned the gene. When you come down, we should be able to determine from her DNA whether or not she has it."

CHAPTER THIRTEEN

[1]

And so they had cloned her gene. Why stop there? Why not clone her stem cells and grow a new kidney? Why not go all the way.

Why not . . . clone Hillary?

The fantasy hit me like a Force Ten cyclone. Here is the perfect situation for a clone: A loving family has a perfectly normal, beautiful child who is struck down at eighteen months by a rare genetic disease that wastes her brains and kidneys. The parents struggle and battle their way through decades of medical crisis, but they long to know what the potential of their child was . . . or is. And so they have Hillary 2 decanted. As hardened veterans of the wars for the handicapped, they battle again through all the ethical elements of the cloning and genetic controversies to secure their second chance.

Here's how the process works: They meander off to the local fertilization laboratory where the virile dad donates his sperm, and the fertile mom donates her eggs. Because they are carriers of the same dread mutation that creates the Schimke disorder, there is a 1 in 4 chance that their mutations will connect again, so the decanter must be careful. On his smudge board he sketches a diagram of the parent's genotype, using small and capital a's and b's.

	B	b
A	AB	Ab
a	aB	ab

That settled, eight petri dishes are arranged. In my medieval sensibility, I require this to be done sensitively. I want the laboratory equivalent of the home-birthing room we had at the county hospital in Durham, North Carolina, for this is the mystical, awesome process of creating a human life. Instead of fluorescent lights and aluminum, candlelight and soft music fill the room, decorated with rocking chairs as a bedroom suite. Of the eight dishes, two are affected by the mutation. We know, because the sperm and eggs in each dish have been screened (and of course, adjusted for the female sex). Closing our eyes and mumbling a chant, we choose one of the unaffected dishes. That dish will be used to create the embryo for Hillary 2.

It could happen differently. At the local hatchery there might still be the eight dishes. But instead of discarding the affected two dishes, the scientists will consult the manual of Dr. Mario Capecchi, and the misspelled DNA that constitutes the mutation will be corrected. "The bat jumped over the moon" will be changed in the dish back to "The cat jumped over the moon." Then all eight petri dishes will be equal and normal. Our choice will be more even-handed, more random and less discriminatory, less sinister.

Of course, some will worry, for political reasons, about how to dispose of the unused petri dishes. To discard . . . or to freeze? I remember the remark of John Finnis, the Oxford don, at the conference in Florence: It is as if little people reside in refrigerators all over America. The question does not engage me emotionally. Do with them what you want, freeze or discard: I don't care. It's a problem for the hatchery administration or for the protesters outside on the street and for congressmen in Washington. It doesn't matter to me.

Maybe we have a third option. Perhaps the hatchery will not need us at all. Perhaps they can work with Hillary alone. We let them swab her cells from her inner mouth, take a plug of skin and a vial of blood, and go to work on her stem cells, tricking them into fertilizing with warm electric light.

And so our situation covers all aspects of the debate. Hillary is the perfect candidate for genetic manipulation, for stem-cell research and human embryo creation, for therapeutic cloning and reproductive cloning. In Hillary 2 we relive her birth but correct the atmospherics. No New York doctor on the phone in the hall this time. We glory in her development beyond eighteen months, watch her grow to be nearly six feet tall, watch her beautiful mind develop. In short, we finally experience the potential of Hillary 1 in Hillary 2. Hillary 2 is the child we were robbed of having.

We cannot be accused of the usual criticisms of cloning. This would be no exercise in eugenics or vanity. We are not trying to clone Michael Jordan, although secretly I would not mind if the gene that governed my soccer prowess at UNC as a youth could be tweaked in the clone, so that she could follow me to UNC and join the undefeated women's soccer team of my old pal Anson Dorrance.

Nor will she, God forbid, be an unloved slave, or an unwilling or unwitting purveyor of body parts. We love Hillary 2 as deeply as we love the original Hillary. She is the perfect sister, with a profound sympathy for her devastated older sister, and with a profound understanding of what Hillary 1 is thinking and feeling. And yes, if someday Hillary's kidney disease grows critical again, perhaps Hillary 2 will want to donate her redundant kidney to her double. Of course, we leave that decision entirely up to the clone.

But wait! Hillary 2 might be genetically identical to Hillary 1, but don't identical twins often have different personalities? Don't they often develop different health problems and die of different causes? Hillary 2 would be growing up in a different time and a different place, with altogether different environmental and cultural influences. What if Hillary 2 turned out to lack the qualities we especially love in the essential Hillary? What if the clone is mean-spirited?

At the Ironworks Barbecue joint in Austin, I float this fantasy for Denise. I know it will have a wallop. She dissolves into sobs, as I fear, and becomes so discombobulated that later in the day she takes Hillary's four o'clock antiseizure medicines by mistake and is bummed out for two days.

[2]

In December 2002 we approached the Texas Medical Center and its Baylor College of Medicine with dizzying awe and trepidation. This world-famous complex of sparkling glass-and-brick towers is the house that Dr. Michael DeBakey built, or so it seemed, for the name of this acclaimed heart surgeon was plastered everywhere. Dr. DeBakey had been the head of surgery at Baylor when he invented his heart pump and when he implanted the first successful artificial heart into a human being in 1966. If I ran into the good doctor in the hallway, I vowed, I would ask him if the idea of building an artificial kidney in his basement had ever occurred to him.

That Dr. Cornelius Boerkoel was also on the Baylor faculty lent him even more luster in our eyes, and we waited patiently for him in a kid-friendly environment of bubbling water tubes, pastel carpets, and building blocks. This lively decor made no impression on Hillary, for she was having a bad day. Our prior communication with the hospital had stressed that this visit was free, since it was for "research purposes," and for the first time in eighteen years, I viewed my daughter fleetingly as a laboratory animal. In Washington our NIH doctor, Dr. Donna Krasnewich, had told us not to be too awed by this visit, for we were doing Dr. Boerkoel a big favor by bringing Hillary to see him.

I expected an elderly man, portly perhaps, mustachioed, with the jolly manner of a pediatrician. Or worse, the consummate scientist with the overbearing self-confidence of a world beater. His medical papers were full of the letters, numbers, and labels like pleiotropic and chromatin remodeling that only an insider could understand, and he had spent a lot of time with fruit flies and mice. He was probably eccentric.

But wait. He had come to his research in genetics circuitously, for he had spent a number of years in Alaska ministering to natives in far-flung villages, frequently flying for hours in Piper Cubs to reach his patients. In 1996 in Toronto, he encountered his first patients with Schimke immuno-osseous dysplasia, siblings who had fought courageously against the scourges of stroke and recurrent infections that this awful, rare disorder presented. Their struggle and their courage had touched him deeply, and he dedicated himself to a search for the source of this unknown and unstudied killer. Over time his net stretched worldwide, from Scotland to Czechoslovakia to Brazil, as he searched in his lab for the genetic mutation that drove the disease.

Instead of a cheek pincher or a blowhard or a weirdo, a slender younger man with curly hair and a careful, halting, almost shy manner presented himself to us. We liked him immediately. On his laptop computer, he showed us pictures of various children, with their bulbous noses like Hillary's and their bowed spines and widely spaced eyes. His sense of caring for these rare sufferers was evident.

There were, he announced at the outset, only fifty-six known cases of Schimke in the world. Only five had lived past the age of fifteen, most having died between the ages of five and ten. We looked over at our child, oblivious and in her tuck on the examining table. Was she really the oldest living Schimke sufferer? All had the severe renal disease of Hillary, he continued, but none were mentally retarded . . . that was not a feature of the disease, no matter what the Johns Hopkins doctor had argued in his medical paper. The disease of all Schimke children was progressive, and they were susceptible to frequent infections and even strokes. Yet Hillary was relatively stable. What did he think of the Johns Hopkins article about Hillary? I asked him early on. He was skeptical, he replied. I smiled to myself.

"Mental retardation is not part of Schimke disease," he said. "But that doesn't mean it can't happen." I drooped.

The two hours we spent with Dr. Boerkoel were cordial, but somber, for this was serious business. He talked of the severe and mild forms of Schimke disease. The severe cases showed nonsense mutation, whereas the mild cases were merely missense mutations. I chuckled. Nonsense or missense? You must be kidding. Were we Alices in Wonderland?

During the visit he paid only deflective attention to Hillary. It was as if he knew what he needed to know about her in his first glance. The lab would tell the tale. Most of our time together was spent looking over his data on his portable computer, or at pictures of his exotic and sometimes grotesque patients. We got another genetics lesson in which the metaphor of misspellings in the genetic code again came into play. More than Denise, I was reasonably sure that my genetic misspellings had caused this terrible condition in my child. Maybe it was not a misspelled sequence that linked to Schimke per se. Maybe not even in the same "pathway" or same "suspect region." But genetic certainly. Foreordained. For some odd psychological reason, this view bound me closer to Hillary. I, rather than some cruel misfortune of incredible bad luck or horrible malpractice, was responsible for her condition.

I had adopted Devin's attitude. We were in this together.

But it was not just a misspelling in the genetic code that was important, Dr. Boerkoel cautioned us, but the reason for the misspelling. Why does this misspelling make her sick? That was the question. Even if he knew what a mutation looked like at a specific location in the human genome, it was not just a matter of changing a single letter or a single word.

"We cannot go about genetic therapy," he said, "until we know why a particular sequence is misspelled." This seemed to complicate the issue.

In due course he took blood from the three of us. In the coming few months, he would examine the DNA he extracted from our blood and look for any nonsense or missense in the SNF2 protein designated as *SMARCAL1* on the genome map. He would be in touch.

We went off for a Vietnamese lunch in something like a state of shock.

[3]

At my obsession to find an answer to the Hillary riddle through genetics, Maeve was in a state of high anxiety. This quest had been revealed to her sometime earlier in the most inopportune way. She had come down from college with her beau, a budding medical student, when Hillary was in Baltimore at the Kennedy Krieger Institute. In an unguarded moment, a doctor had discussed the possibility of a genetic explanation for Hillary's condition in the presence of the college sweethearts, and Maeve flew out of the room in tears.

"No one will ever want to marry me now," she murmured. To his credit her boyfriend took her in his arms and disabused her of the notion that this would affect their relationship in any way.

If Hillary had the bad seed, Maeve had a 67 percent chance of being a carrier, for genetic disorders are transmitted through the family. But this sounds more daunting than it really is. It did not seem to calm Maeve down to know that her mate would have to have the very same bad seed for them to create a Schimke baby. The chance of two lovers having the same misspelled DNA at the same pinprick in the human genome is extremely remote.

Dr. Krasnewich at NIH had offered to provide genetic counseling for Maeve during this delicate state, but Maeve had resisted. The offer smacked of the dilemma of HIV testing: Did Maeve really want to know?

"I would never want Hillary's condition to interfere with love," Dr. Krasnewich had said, "just because the man gets nervous. But if Maeve were to get married and wanted to have children, she should definitely have genetic counseling beforehand, mainly to eliminate any fears that are not borne out by facts."

[4]

A few months after our Texas visit, in late February 2002, I received an e-mail from Dr. Boerkoel. "A few weeks ago," it said, "I completed the sequencing of the *SMARCAL1* exons in Hillary's DNA and both of your DNAs. I did *not* find any mutations in this gene. This testing does not exclude some mutations such as large deletions or rearrangements. However, this is the extent of the testing that I am able to offer at this time. This result makes the diagnosis of Schimke immuno-osseous dysplasia much less likely, but cannot exclude the diagnosis."

He sent the scientific results in an attachment, and I immediately forwarded them to our adviser at NIH. By independent confirmation, Boerkoel's DNA study met the gold standard of genetic medicine. Despite his careful disclaimers about "large deletions and rearrangements" in Hillary's genetic code—a highly remote possibility—we were to regard this as "powerful evidence."

"Your message was received here with a strange combination of disappointment and relief," I replied. That was my own reaction, whereas Denise had let out a whoop of joy. I longed for a certainty I could deal with, some definitive answer after so long and frustrating a quest. It went to the power of knowing, or should I say, the powerlessness of not knowing. So the bat had not jumped over the moon, after all. We were not to know what had jumped over what, if anything indeed had, or where the risky feat had taken place, if indeed it had. It seemed more than likely now that we were never to know. We had taken the old and the new medicine as far as they could go, but they could provide not even the first clue. We were only allowed to know what she did not have.

Several weeks later, we had a long telephone conversation with Dr. Boerkoel, who had now become something of a semideity in our household. He walked us methodically through his testing procedure, how he applied the well-known polymerase chain reaction (PCR) test, often used in forensic genetics, to the eighteen base pairs or exons of Hillary's DNA in the *SMARCAL1* region. His "proofreading" of these base pairs uncovered no errors.

Then he had examined our DNA and again found no abnormalities. He checked and rechecked, moved to the edges and beyond of this suspect genetic span. In scientific parlance, there were no errors in the message.

No hoary bats flitted about where only cats were supposed to be.

Of the bad seed of Schimke immuno-osseous dysplasia, we were all clean.

CHAPTER FOURTEEN

———————

[1]

In the summer of 2002, I turned my attention vigorously back to the transplant front. There I was not powerless. Dr. K had suggested the "squeaky-wheel" approach, and I was ready to do some squeaking. Denise and I had to acknowledge to each other that our girl was sliding downhill. She had very little energy and seemed to want only to sleep most of the time. The Unsinkable Molly Brown was sinking. She was withdrawing, as if she was entering some sort of final phase.

If I was prepared once again to be the hysterical father with Hillary's transplant doctors, I had also acquired, in my despair over whether Hillary would ever get the call, a healthy curiosity about alternative sources for organs that might become possible in the very near future. About just how far away the world was from human clones or stem-cell miracles or animal organs fit for transplant from other species into humans, I had no illusions. Hillary's problems had come thirty years too early, and I wondered if America, for political or moral reasons, would ever countenance transspecies or clone-bred cures.

But her case led to dreams and fantasies, and these futuristic remedies were not entirely academic. If she were to get a human transplant soon, it might wear out in ten years and have to be replaced. What then? The miracles of the future seemed to hover just over the horizon: the day when a kidney could be grown from a stem cell in a petri dish, or taken from a human clone in a clone slave camp, or, most promisingly, harvested from a transgenic nude pig. If science proved these solutions to be safe, morals and politics would eventually be shoved aside. It had happened that way with in vitro fertilization.

From both an intellectual and moral perspective, the unnaturalness of these miracle cures gnawed at me. I needed to make up my mind. The issue had to be defined starkly: If Hillary was about to die, could I overcome my ethical qualms and accept a clone's kidney or a pig organ? In an industry poll, 70 percent of the American public had said they would, provided the organ was safe and functional. *Provided* was the operative word.

At my conference in Florence several years before, a French sociologist, Dominique Mehl, had spoken of the panic that the birth of Dolly the sheep had created in Catholic France in the winter of 1997. "What had just happened in Scotland," Dr. Mehl said of the French panic, "is inconceivable, unacceptable, intolerable. The issue is not worth discussing. The only suitable reaction was that of immediate prohibition."

But further research had not been prohibited. And public attitudes had progressed far down the road in the four years after Dolly. Pigs and rabbits and cows and even mules had been cloned, a veritable animal farm of unnatural creatures. The procedure was getting more efficient with each passing year. President Bush had not banned the process of "nuclear transfer" (cloning) altogether, as he might have; he only denied federal funding for certain types of stem-cell research. By 2002 many in the scientific community felt that human cloning was not only possible, but expected in the next few years. It would probably happen offshore, but it would happen. By ten years, the wealthy would be using human cloning routinely, to engineer the kind of children they wanted. The doctors who helped these patients would be lionized rather than reviled. And they would be rich.

And so I got in the car and drove five hours to Blacksburg, Virginia, where the American subsidiary of the Roslin Institute, the group that cloned Dolly, had its laboratory. It was now called PPL Therapeutics. At its eight-hundred-acre farm not far from the Virginia Tech campus, PPL had followed Dolly with the first cloned piglets in 2000 and then the first transgenic cloned pigs in 2002. The latter were the nude pigs that had been stripped immunologically of the gene that defined their species. As a gift to the new millennium, two of the five had been named Millie and Dotcom. These nude creatures had not only had their pig gene "knocked out" of their DNA, but in place of the knocked-out gene, a human gene had been added. It was hoped that this swap would address the problem of rejection.

The last hurdle was safety. Beyond the problem of rejection, was it possible that the process of transplanting organs across the species divide could produce catastrophic new diseases—in short, the new AIDS? For AIDS was an endogenous disease, residing in the genes, and it was now established that AIDS had come into the human race from monkeys. The porcine version of this dread prospect was called PERV (porcine endogenous retrovirus). Unless the risk of unique retroviruses could be completely eliminated, xenotransplantation had no future.

At a purple office building, just past the cavernous football stadium where the flashy Michael Vick had thrilled his fans on his championship teams for the Virginia Tech Hokies, Dr. David Ayares, the research director for PPL and its master manipulator, greeted me warily. A tall, broad-shouldered man with a scientist's flat delivery, he looked tired, for he'd been on the road continually in the previous months trying to drum up investment money for the xenotransplantation program. Investors in his "preclinical" phase had been hard to convince. "We're a twenty-million-dollar company, and as yet have no product," he said. But he was dangling the prospect of a $5 billion market in solid organs alone, if PPL's research paid off over the next six years.

"There are eighty thousand people on the waiting lists now," he said. "Sixteen die every day for lack of an organ. The availability of human organs is growing more scarce. And the list is growing, primarily because, with air bags and seat belts, road safety has improved." I had never before linked better highway safety with fewer transplant organs. Now I understood why a transplant doctor had referred to motorcycles as "donormobiles."

Americans are loath to promise their organs in the event of accidental death, Dr. Ayares pointed out. This hesitation contrasts with countries such as the Netherlands, Sweden, and Spain, where organ donations are immediate and expected and required by law.

In the course of my three-hour visit at PPL, it seemed as if Dr. Ayares was intent on breaking down my skepticism about xenotransplantation. Pig parts, especially tissue and fluids, had been utilized in American medicine for decades. To benefit the more than 3 million diabetics in America, pig insulin has been used for twenty-five years. In Mexico doctors were experimenting with implanting pig islet cells in the body of diabetics to produce insulin, and with this experimental therapy, there had been no evidence of a retrovirus. By producing a safe transgenic pig as a source of replacement parts, hearts could be grown to size and specification, like parts for a

Saturn car. Stem cells from pigs could help burn victims; pig dopamine could be manufactured for Alzheimer's sufferers. Muhammad Ali, a Muslim who, for religious reasons, ate no pork, had undergone an experimental therapy for his Parkinson's disease in which pig cells were injected into his brain, in the hope that they would make dopamine. That experiment did not improve the champ's condition, but neither had there been evidence of infection with a porcine retrovirus.

In mid-2002 PPL was six months away from experimental surgery on a baboon. The primate would receive a kidney from a nude pig, and an immunosuppressant "cocktail" slightly different from the one a human would receive. The company would then take data for two years. If all went well at that phase, the clinical phase would begin with human volunteers.

"Like Hillary?" I asked.

He nodded, but did not seem to want to personalize.

After these steps satisfied the Food and Drug Administration, he expected PPL to be on the market in 2008. A new vision of the animal farm was emerging. In ten years a farm for cloned, transgenic pigs would abut every major transplant center, like Pittsburgh, Miami, or Iowa City. With the process safe and perfected, his company would create a herd of 120 "founder animals" with the engineered gene. From that founder herd, standard breeding practices would take over. In only four years, Dr. Ayares proclaimed, a herd of 100,000 genetically engineered nude pigs was possible.

For my long five-hour drive home, this was a lot to think about. As I settled into my thoughts and started past Roanoke, where two interstate highways come together, I suddenly caught sight out of the corner of my eye of a battered white pickup truck bounding over the median strip and careening directly across the highway in front of me. Fortunately, there was a gap in the traffic. As I flew past the truck, I saw it crash into the bank on the side of the highway, its windshield and side windows shattering. Then a man fell out of the side, scrambling away from his wreck. Undoubtedly, he had survived because he was wearing his seat belt.

[2]

In the five years that Hillary had waited on the Virginia transplant list, from 1993 to 1998, she had gotten close to being the recipient only a few times. In virtually every instance she was called, she was designated as the second or third backup for a fresh kidney that had just arrived from some mysterious source. In each of these calls, we were asked to rush to the closest hospital for fresh blood work so that her values could be compared with the available organ. Then we had to wait, usually through the night, to know whether this would truly be our moment and Hillary's deliverance, or yet another disappointment.

These episodes took on a certain dull and frustrating pattern. Usually, we tossed and turned throughout the night, and then the phone rang in the early morning with the news, always delivered in the flat tone of mock sorrow, that the "prime candidate" had indeed received the precious kidney. Or we were informed that Hillary's blood had proved to be incompatible with the donor's. Once Hillary was actually admitted into the hospital as a surgery patient, only to be told to go home after a stay of five hours.

Why was Hillary always the bridesmaid and never the bride? I harbored a deep suspicion that something fishy was going on, especially when year after year went by, until she achieved the dubious standing of being the suppliant who had been the longest on everyone's list. She was being passed over, I became more and more convinced, because she was handicapped. This gnawing suspicion made me furious, and I dared any doctor or institution to give me the least hard evidence for my suspicion.

When I confronted the doctors with this not-so-veiled charge of discrimination, they denied it. Perhaps discrimination was the dirty secret of the old days, they would say, when the list contained real names, the situation of the person was known, and hospital ethics committees made the final determination. But that system had been changed. Like it or not, the list was now simply a list of numbers. The better the match, the quicker the transplant. Because Hillary's medical history was complicated, it was hard to find a proper match for her. In this crapshoot, clearly we weren't very good at craps.

In the spring of 2002, an episode took place that put me over the top. Yet again the phone rang and the voice from across the river said that a kidney was available. They were listing Hillary as "first backup." Two things were different this time, however. The donor was not a victim but a saint, a thirty-eight-year-old living woman who wished, out of her sheer love of humanity, to donate one of her kidneys. Second, something really different, Hillary was compatible with this donor's blood and tissue type. She was a match, not a perfect one perhaps, but sufficiently so. Then came the wrinkle. The primary candidate was a two-year-old child. As if to offer me encouragement, the nurse said that the transplant doctors were not sure that the plumbing could be made to work when a thirty-eight-year-old kidney was stuffed into a two-year-old's body. So there was a good chance that Hillary would move from backup to starter.

I hit the roof. Do you mean to say that when my child, after eight years of waiting, is finally found to be compatible with a living donor, she is listed as a backup to a two-year-old? I was incredulous. Where was the humanity and the decency in this? The nurse mumbled some blandishment. Nevertheless, "we need for Hillary to get some blood drawn," she said flatly. I refused. Call us if the prime candidate does not get the kidney, I said. We will take no more backup calls. And I slammed the receiver down. I did not even tell Denise about the call.

It was to get worse. The prime candidate, as usual, got the kidney, but, miracle of modern pipe fitting that it was, the surgery made the local news. The story had a curious human-interest angle as well. The family of the two-year-old was of Arab extraction, and, the announcer stated, this Muslim family had a religious principle against giving a kidney, but none against taking one. America was still in the grip of its post–September 11 anger. Anti-Arab and anti-Muslim sentiment pervaded the national mood. I had been arguing against this bias whenever I spoke in public about my new book on the Third Crusade, *Warriors of God.* But after this story, I had to work hard to keep my own resentment at bay.

More important, I resented a system of organ donation that was so oblivious to the human equation. Why had no doctor stepped forward to advocate for Hillary? How could two years on the list trump eight? On the afternoon when the choice of the recipient was in the balance, none of Hillary's doctors would take my call. It was all a matter of cold numbers, and the Arab child's biological numbers must have been marginally better than Hillary's. At the next regular meeting with Hillary's kidney doctors, I went out of my way to tell them that I thought their system of organ distribution stank.

[3]

We had become gamblers and whiners and politicians: gamblers in a crapshoot; whiners in an endless pursuit against terrible odds and pitted against families in equally desperate circumstances; politicians trying to bend an impersonal system to our own personal interest. In 2001, 52,766 people waited for a kidney transplant, and only 5,803 scored with the organ of a dead person. By the calculation of Dr. Ayares at PPL, nearly 6,000 people died every year for lack of an organ. As each year passed without a transplant, Hillary appeared to be dwindling, her dialysis seeming to work less and less efficiently, her smiles a rare occurrence because she obviously felt so lousy all the time.

In 1999, nervous and resentful, we took our biggest gamble of all. After five years of this backup madness in Virginia, I read a story in *USA Today* that suggested the "list" moved more quickly in the Midwest. The country is divided into eleven regions. Our Region 11 encompassed Virginia, the Carolinas, Kentucky, and Tennessee, and was dotted with ten "organ procurement centers." But Region 8, encompassing Iowa, Missouri, Kansas, Nebraska, Colorado, and Wyoming, had only four procurement centers, the most important being in Iowa City, Iowa. There, *USA Today* reported, the average wait was less than two years.

Why not shift Hillary's points for time onto the list to Iowa? In December 2000 I took her to Iowa City to explore the possibility. With lovely art on its walls and constant smiles on empathetic faces everywhere, the University of Iowa Hospital impressed immediately. After much prodding and pushing on her belly, the transplant doctor finally turned to me and said that they would accept her onto the Iowa list.

"It's the humane thing to do," he said.

Perhaps I should not have been so struck by that phrase. The humane thing to do? No doctor in Washington had ever used that term. I came back a great Iowa booster, a secret Hawkeye, excited about the prospects, wallowing in my own Midwestern ancestry, and indulging in some black humor about how a good, healthy, corn-fed kidney was just what the doctor was ordering for Hillary.

And so we made the switch. Iowa would be our primary list, and Virginia would become secondary. Then two years rolled by without a peep from Iowa. Had we made another tactical mistake? Was Hillary really on their screen out there? It was time for some straight talk.

On July 16, 2002, Hillary had her annual visit with her transplant doctor in Virginia. He was an amiable Icelander, Dr. Johann Jonsson, whom I liked immensely. He played an abysmal game of golf, partly because he always had a cell phone in his ear. He and I had engaged in some light banter about my research trips to the Viking sites of Iceland for my book on the millennium. After I blurted out my frustrations about the silence of Iowa, Dr. Jonsson allowed that perhaps it was time to "bring her back home." He meant bringing her points back to her local area, making Virginia once again her primary list. Before we did anything precipitous, he promised to call Iowa and determine Hillary's status out there. I will always believe that it was this call of Dr. Jonsson's that turned Hillary's fortunes.

During that conversation, I asked Jonsson how long a good kidney might be expected to last if Hillary were actually transplanted. The average survival rate was ten years, he said.

"And then?" I asked.

"And then we might be able to grow her a kidney in a dish." He was an optimist about the speed of stem-cell research and its general acceptance by politicians and the public. But I found his remark immensely comforting. If we could ever get Hillary off this infernal transplant list, I was determined that she would never, ever go back on it.

CHAPTER FIFTEEN

[1]

On July 17 I drove to Baltimore for a colonoscopy. Home in the early afternoon, feeling lousy and a bit sorry for myself, I shooed Denise and Hillary out of the house and went to bed for a few hours. At 5:30 p.m. I was awakened by the phone. At the voice on the other end, I sat bolt upright. It was Barbara Schanbacher, the transplant coordinator at the University of Iowa Hospital. I'd talked to her the day before, as had Dr. Jonsson. She knew that we were thinking about severing our relationship with Iowa.

"This is a miracle," she said, "but we'd like to offer Hillary a kidney." Could we get her out to Iowa by midnight?

I stammered a yes, hung up the phone in shock, and sprang into action. What planes? What to pack? And hey, where was Hillary? I thought I remembered Denise talking about taking her kayaking on the river. But where? I imagined two happy sunset gazers, paddling away the precious few hours we had before the last plane to Cedar Rapids. I called boathouses. I called Maeve in Austin, and, phone master that she is, she went operational. And then, twenty minutes later, they surfaced. It was a blistering hot day in Washington, and they had bagged the river in favor of a movie, *The Bourne Identity,* because Hillary found Matt Damon so devilishly cute.

On the phone Denise hyperventilated her joy and disbelief. I, in turn, presented myself as a picture of composure.

"Just get home as soon as you can . . . and drive safely," I said.

Just past 8 p.m., we arrived at the Baltimore/Washington International Airport, confident with forty minutes to spare. At the counter, the horse-faced clerk was adamant as she glared at her unforgiving computer screen. The flight was closed. Didn't we know to allow an hour and a half in the post–September 11 environment? she scolded. There was nothing she could do. Regulations and procedures, you know. She could not accept our bags. The new federal agents at the security checkpoint would never let us through. We would have to go tomorrow. She looked past us to her next victim. Denise threw a fit.

"We have waited for eight years for this kidney, and you are not going to stop us," she said fiercely.

The clerk shrugged her shoulders and gave us the tickets and we bolted for security, with Hillary perched pashalike on our lumpy suitcases and her "kid," the dialysis machine. I had wanted to leave the kid at home not to jinx us, but Barb Schanbacher had told me to bring it, just in case things didn't work out. "Just in case . . ." The words lingered.

BWI had become a nightmare after September 11, a horror show of endless lines snaking through the corridors and constant shouting matches between airport security officers and frazzled travelers. They had finally resorted to hiring clowns to calm the ferocious mob. I looked at my watch. We were down to twenty minutes before flight time. I had my doubts. The new federal agents were in their first week of official service. They were bound to be picky.

At the metal detectors, we blurted out our situation. To our astonishment the new G-men mobilized around us like beavers, as if we represented just the situation they had trained for days before. Bags flew open and shut. Hillary was wheeled through, cooing happily. My tennis shoes came off and went back on in a jiffy. All the time the agents dispensed comforting words. Don't worry, our gate was just around the corner. We can do this. Minutes later, pondering the dichotomy of narrow-minded clerks and bighearted G-men in this world, we fell into our seats in exhausted euphoria. Hillary looked at us quizzically. Were we crazy? What was all the fuss about? Another plane ride. Whoopee.

Was our nightmare really over? Did we dare dream of this as the turning point? As Hillary fell asleep across her mother's lap, Denise did dare, more than I. From her purse she pulled the page from the end of *The Great Gatsby* that she always kept close by for profound junctures in her life: ". . . tomorrow we will run faster, stretch out our arms farther . . ." I could not let myself go. For too long I had steeled myself for bad news. Now I would live only in this enchanted moment and let tomorrow bring whatever it would bring, even the "vast obscurity" of which Fitzgerald wrote at the end, as we were drawn not to a new day, but "borne back ceaselessly into the past."

Four hours later, not long after midnight, we strolled out of the Cedar Rapids airport and took our first deep breath of the soft night air of Iowa. We could smell the corn growing just over the airport fence, and as we drove to Iowa City, flashes of lightning lit up the night sky far in the distance.

[2]

The night was filled with the usual tests and consultations, as the endless parade of doctors, nurses, and technicians, needles hovering like weapons, traipsed through the room. It felt a little like a space shuttle launch. We were T minus eleven hours. Liftoff was scheduled for 2 p.m.

the next day, and the countdown was proceeding nominally. But I knew from the shuttle launches I had attended in the 1980s that a mission can be scrubbed at T minus three seconds before main engine start. I could not shake my pessimism.

By morning a sense of inevitability hovered in the air. To assuage our anxieties about the surgery, doctors explained that installing a kidney was a far-easier procedure than harvesting one. The horror would be a rejection right on the surgeon's table, when a mismatched kidney could turn black before the surgeon's eyes and shrivel up like a prune. But none of them had ever seen that happen, and they were sure that this was no mismatch. Hillary's post-transplant nephrologist briefed us about how our life would change after surgery. Medicine had perfected its antirejection drugs, the soft-spoken and amiable and reassuring Dr. Craig Porter told us. Technically, Hillary would be at high risk for rejection in the first six months, but nowadays, he said, they put the words "high risk" in quotes.

At 1 p.m. all the results were back; we were cleared for launch. Hillary needed to be bathed. Not far from her room was a deep bath, where we scrubbed and coiffed her as if she was headed for a debutante ball. For good measure, Denise shaved her armpits and legs. In a side table we found stickers, some of which were printed with the word *awesome,* so we decorated her shoulders with them like epaulets. The gurney arrived promptly at 2 p.m., spread out with forest-green sheets, and Hillary climbed happily aboard. Because she had no sense of anticipation, she could have no dread. She was taking her emotional cues from us, and we were giggling and babbling like idiots.

I pulled the gurney from the front. Halfway down the hallway toward the surgery suite, I turned around and noticed that Denise was nowhere in sight. We tarried for a minute, and she soon reappeared from around a corner, tears streaming down her cheeks, and holding a box marked "Organ/tissue for transplant." It was an ordinary cardboard box, lined with well-cleaned Styrofoam. On its top were the words "Perishable. This side up." It had been discarded in the hallway, waiting for the janitor. If Hannah Arendt could write about the banality of evil, this was surely the banality of good. We kept it, and later, I thought, I would give it to a sculptor friend to transform into a work of art.

In the ready room the anesthesiologists took over. One of them, a pert young doctor, asked about nicknames, and finally, taking note of her stickers, settled on calling her "Awesome Hillary." Then they wheeled her through the glass doors.

Hillary never looked back.

[3]

Four hours later the transplant surgeon, Dr. Stephen Rayhill, appeared in his green scrubs to proclaim the procedure a resounding success. The kidney had been nearly as good as if it had come from a family member, he said.

Hillary was peeing like crazy. We never imagined that we could get so excited about urine.

In the days ahead, as Hillary recovered first in the intensive care unit and later in her own room, our spirits soared. We were riding a magic carpet. The experience was profound, on the level of the birth of our first child.

And I became fixated with the donor. Details drifted our way. The donor had been an eighteen-year-old high-school graduate. He had been a young man of great promise. He was a star athlete and fine student. His death had been a tragedy that had shocked his Iowa county, somewhere north of Iowa City.

I was entering a delicate area, for I had long since realized that if Hillary were ever transplanted, our joy would be linked to someone else's grief. In the exchange of a human organ, death and life are inextricably linked in a miracle of modern science. For eight years Hillary, the potential "recipient," had to wait for just the right "donor" of a cadaveric organ. Now those impersonal words had become intensely personal and human and real. Of course, I understood why the language was impersonal. Many families could not bear to think about the source of the life-giving organ. It was too much to think of oneself as the joyous beneficiary of another's horrible tragedy. The gender of an organ was not masculine or feminine, but neuter. Would "it" function properly? Was "it" a good match? For those in need of anonymity and distance, the depersonalization was necessary as a deliverance from guilt.

My instinct was different. I wanted to know . . . I had to know . . . Who was this spectacular donor? To know became a compulsion. In so intimate a gift, I was in awe.

"You've probably read the papers," Barb Schanbacher said as we skirted around this uncomfortable question a few days after Hillary's surgery.

It was true. From the snippets of information I'd gotten from the doctors, I had enough to do my own search, first in the local paper, then to a town library in Monticello, Iowa, sixty miles north of Iowa City. Then to that town's newspaper, the *Monticello Express*. Hillary's benefactor was Jared Gassmann, a high school football star and top student who had been killed in a race of four-wheel all-terrain vehicles (ATVs) at the Jones County Fair. His obituary focused on the remarkable catches he used to make as a wide receiver, fifteen yards down the field when it was third and ten.

MONTICELLO, IOWA—An 18 year old Monticello man was killed on Tuesday, July 16, during the motocross race at the Great Jones County Fair.

Jared Gassmann was injured when he lost control of his all-terrain vehicle during the motocross race at approximately 7:30 p.m. Gassmann was taken to the University of Iowa Hospitals and Clinics via helicopter after the accident where he later died from his injuries.

This was the first time all-terrain vehicles were added to the motocross, and the accident was not anything expected by the fair organizers, John Harms, fair manager, said.

"Nothing like this has ever happened," Harms said.

MONTICELLO—Law enforcement officials and Jones County Fair Board members plan to meet to discuss the fatal accident at an all-terrain vehicle race on July 16.

Jones County Sheriff Mark Denniston said his department wasn't aware of the accident that killed Jared Gassmann, 18, of Monticello, until the next morning.

Paramedics at the scene radioed an emergency helicopter to take Gassmann to University Hospitals in Iowa City.

John Harms, Jones County Fair director, said the emergency crews that needed to be at the race were there and an investigation wasn't necessary.

"This event was not a wrongdoing event," he said. "It's not something that was illegal or immoral or anything that needs to have any kind of policing or sheriff review to have to exist or continue with. It's a very everyday event."

—NEWS ACCOUNTS

In those first few weeks after surgery, this profound connection of life and death kept us oscillating between laughter and tears.

Almost from the first hours after she awakened from the ether of the operating room, a new Hillary emerged. For more than a year, we had scarcely gotten a smile from her. The frown on her brow, the clearest message we had of how she felt, was almost permanent. Now she was constant smiles. They were almost goofy in nature at first, as if she could not believe what she was feeling. And we felt like going into a hip-swaying jive at the words "I feel good . . . dooda . . . doooda . . . dooo." During the first day, she was up and walking the halls, even as we winced at the incision that stretched from below her breast to her pelvis. Later we consigned this burst of energy to steroids, and imagined the muscles that would soon follow. We regarded her with astonishment. How could we have been so stupid? We had been deprived of her true sunny nature all this time, solely because she was suffering. Suddenly, miraculously, she was liberated from pain.

Before we left Iowa, Hillary and I made a pilgrimage to Monticello. On the outskirts of the farm town of three thousand, past the implement business with its gigantic combines and massive tractors, a billboard advertised the just-completed 150th Great Jones County Fair. "The best five days of summer" was its slogan. At the first convenience store, I found an old flyer listing the events for July 16, including "The Motocross 'Bud Run': motorcycles and quads!" and the evening concert featuring Aaron Tippin and that old favorite of country, George Jones, who would be performing songs from his new album, *Cold Hard Truth*.

It was now nearly three weeks after the accident. The *Monticello Express* carried a special section on the events at the Great Jones County Fair. All the winners were pictured with their prize bulls and guinea pigs and champion swine. But there was no mention of the biggest loser at the fair. Except in the classified section. There, in a section slugged "Card of Thanks," was a letter from Jared Gassmann's grandmother: "I would like to thank Jared on behalf of Grandpa Frank Fitzsimmons for always helping to keep his cars running, all the movies of his early years and until Jared quit with sports and Christmas plays, also for always keeping him in glasses, finally got contacts that didn't hurt his eyes."

I drove slowly past the shops on Main Street until I happened onto the modest front for Gassmann's Satellite and Security Service. Beyond were pleasant neighborhoods of brick streets and comfortable homes with sweeping porches, reminiscent of my grandparents' home in Sycamore, Illinois. I went to the Methodist church to find its doors locked. Across the street I noticed a man working on his flower bed. I inquired if he knew where the minister of the church lived. It was too far. I paused, unsure of whether I should confess the nature of our visit.

Holding tightly to Hillary's hand, I blurted out, "I'm interested in the tragedy of the Gassmann boy." Did he know which church the family belonged to? The Catholic church, he answered, and pointed out to me the imposing double spires that rose just above the nearby houses. He knew the Gassmanns well. Their house was just over the hill. Did I want to go there? I shook my head. His daughter, he said, was in Jared's class. And he had himself been a witness to the accident.

"How did it happen?" I mumbled.

"It happened right at the start of the race," he said. "When the pack came over the first hill, Jared was slightly ahead. Once over, he seemed to duck down and hit his brake to slow down, and the ATVs behind came flying over that first hill, left the ground, and hit him in the back of the head. You know, those four-wheelers are all bunched together in those races. When they laid him out and blew up those plastic bubbles to stabilize his head, I knew it was bad."

The doors to the Catholic church were open. There, I quietly paid my respects.

[4]

As I was nurturing Hillary back to health in Iowa City, I wrote an article for the *New York Times* about the experience. I was eager to make the point that until stem-cell research or clones or nude pigs could give us Aldous Huxley's vision of a well-stocked "organ store in the sub-basement" of every hospital, families on the transplant list faced the horrible prospect of waiting for someone else's tragedy. I praised the nobility of a victim's family, who, in the midst of shock and grief over a death, had the presence of mind and the generosity to give life to strangers far away. I did not mention Jared Gassmann by name. I gave the article the John O'Hara–like title of "Appointment in Iowa City," for a benign rather than sinister fate had smiled upon us there. Upon its publication the

Times changed the title to "When Generosity Is a Medical Necessity."

The response was great. I heard from many friends and strangers. A man from New York wrote happily that his third kidney transplant had just celebrated "its" twentieth birthday, and his doctors had told him that it would outlive him. A California doctor chided me for my ethical qualms over placing pigs' kidneys in humans. "I no more would be troubled that a loved one had turned into a pig with a xeno transplant than I would that he had turned into someone of the other sex with a transplant from a parent or a sib," she wrote.

Five days after the article appeared, the *Times* carried a series of letters about the piece. The president of a New York organ-donation network, addressing my point about the dehumanized vocabulary of the transplant industry, wrote, "We have changed our terminology to describe the process more sensitively. We prefer 'recovery of organ' to 'harvesting' and 'deceased donor' to 'cadaveric.'" The father of a victim of the terrorist violence in Israel spoke of his establishment of a network for Jewish donors called the Halachic Organ Donor Society "in an attempt to educate religiously observant Jews about the permissibility of organ donation, something that is still not widely understood." A doctor from Washington suggested that donors of organs be "rewarded with a preference in the event that they need an organ themselves."

Several days later I heard from the reporter from the

Cedar Rapids Gazette who had covered the accident at the Great Jones County Fair. He proposed now to write about our two families. "It's unusual," he said breezily, "that you can get both sides of a transplant." I was skeptical, not wanting to cause any further pain to the Gassmann family. Oh, no, the reporter responded, he had already talked to the Gassmanns, and they were eager for the article to be written. And so I agreed to be interviewed. After we spoke on the roof of the University of Iowa Hospital, the reporter gave me the Gassmanns' e-mail address. They had wanted me to have it.

In the article, Jared's father, David Gassmann, expressed the anguish of the family's decision to donate.

"It's not easy to do," he said. "You don't want anyone touching him. When you know he's really gone, that was the hard part, letting him go." (Later, I heard how a doctor in Wisconsin handles his advocacy. To families of the victim, he says, "We can take the body to the morgue right now, or we can make a stop along the way to the morgue and save seven lives.")

I, in turn, used the article to step up on my soapbox yet again about the value of handicapped people. The reporter, who was black, had prodded me with the perfectly legitimate question of whether it was right to give preciously scarce organs to handicapped persons. As one who had no doubt experienced discrimination in his life at some point, he was offering up a home-run ball.

"I would challenge anybody who says handicapped

people are less entitled to organ donation than anybody else," I said.

The *Times* and *Gazette* articles led soon after to an exchange between the families. Denise wrote:

"I cannot delay in expressing our deep sadness at the death of your son. He must have been a terrific kid, and I cannot begin to appreciate what you have lost. Our little Hillary was once very close to dying. . . . It was then I made my pact with God that if he would let Hillary live, I would never again complain about the stroke that took away her language. I know of nothing that remotely approaches the loss of a child. I so wish there was something we could do to help. We are awed and humbled by your tremendous generosity at a moment of such loss. It is really Godlike. There is no greater gift to give than what you both and Jared gave our Hillary."

Five days later, Dave Gassmann replied.

"I do believe that Jared is feeling good that it was your daughter who received his kidney. I say this because Jared always stood up for underdogs. I'm thinking of one particular time when a person in his school was the target of so much harassment at school and after school that the kid's mother was at the point of moving the kid to a school in another town. Jared was very popular and very respected at school. He wasn't very big but he knew his older brother Jordan would stand by him if needed. Anyway, Jared confronted several groups of school kids and told them to back off, that this kid was a friend of his. It made an unbelievable change in the kid's life. That was three years ago.

"People have been asking me if it was a hard decision to donate Jared's organs. The answer is yes. It was the hardest, most painful decision we have ever faced. The thing is, in our case, the real question was 'are you ready to give up on your son's chances for living?'

"Even though the doctors are telling us Jared is brain-dead and will die as soon as they take him off life support, we are still praying to God for a miracle. When we finally came to this unbearable conclusion that God was taking our son, and his pain was over, we knew that Jared would have wanted to do the right thing and help somebody else. . . .

"I hope and pray that Hillary will have a happy and healthy life."

CHAPTER SIXTEEN

On December 1, 2002, Hillary Rory McTier Reston, the erstwhile Fireworks, became an adult. For a few weeks we would set aside any worries about the future that stretched out uncertainly before her—and before us. We would pause, mark the moment, and concentrate on her first twenty-one years. Our blessings were many and profound.

The arc of Hillary's life, dramatic as it was, had been more of an upside-down parabola than an arc. She was now on a spectacular upswing, and we could scarcely contain our joy. Out of the mine shaft, we were swinging giddily on our laser beam to the sky. For months after her transplant, she faced the world with a perpetual smile, as if she were eager to compress into a few months all the health she now suddenly felt, and to make up for the chronic pain she had been suffering for as long as she could remember. More than that, her true self was reemerging: a happy, enthusiastic, sociable, playful, strong-willed, impish, and lively character with true charisma who spread love and fun wherever she went.

Her teachers at school watched this change in awe. Hillary was connected and available and perpetually energetic. Reports of new things that she was doing came back in her school backpack almost daily. She began to eat ravenously. At last I could retire my hated role as her force-feeder. Gone were the diet restrictions and the artificial supplements and horse-pill vitamins, and my physical restraint of her, as I tried to connect with her weaving mouth. Rather, we had to protect our own plates at dinner now, lest she snatch away our piece of meat in good boardinghouse fashion. In the first three months after Iowa City, she gained sixteen pounds. Her body began to feel solid and even muscular, and there were bad jokes about the steroids she was on. Of all things, we began to think about putting her on a diet. Her immunosuppressants, especially the prednisone, gave her a puffy moon face, but we were assured that that would gradually disappear as we walked her medicines down with time.

I could also retire as the family night watchman. With glee, we canned the bedside listening device that had been at my ear throughout the night for years, as I listened for her to stir with a seizure or a dialysis complication. Ceremoniously, we chucked out the boxes of dialysis fluid that had clogged our basement for the past eight years. Could it be that we had had our last emergency trip to the hospital at 3 a.m.? We were afraid to express a happy thought out loud, lest we jinx ourselves.

With her hearty eating and, yes, natural urination, her eyes glowed, her hair glistened with protein-rich highlights, and her complexion took on a luminous cast. It was the return of the famous milky Leary skin, Denise announced unabashedly, giving all the credit to her father and his Irish genes. Irish genes always trumped Scottish ones in our house.

We began to dream, imagining trips all of us could now make . . . perhaps that float trip down the Colorado River without having to think about dialysis supplies and insidious microbes that might infect Hillary's belly. Perhaps we would take her to Tibet and let the Dalai Lama look deeply into her soul. Or go on the much discussed trip to Ireland. We would explore Hillary's druid roots. Denise had a shaky theory about Hillary's "racial memory." I was willing to test it . . . so long as I could also golf along the seaside cliffs of Waterville.

The transformation in Denise went in tandem with Hillary's. Since 1983 she had carried within her a leaden, suffocating, seemingly permanent sadness, as the mother of a chronically ill child. Helplessly, she had looked on and watched her child suffer. But in the colorful fall days of 2002, her desperation, her frustration, her anger seemed to drift away like autumn leaves. I could hear her downstairs, puttering happily around Hillary's room, and singing along with Joan Baez—". . . all my troubles, Lord, will soon be over . . ."—as Hillary chimed in. Our relationship in turn soared. About the life-and-death decisions we had often pondered, reasonable people could disagree, and we had disagreed often, and often unreasonably. A magical serenity descended upon the house.

Maeve and Devin, in turn, seemed at last able to get on with their lives, even to reflect sentimentally and wryly about their crisis-filled childhood. Devin luxuriated in the fact that he had lugged his last dialysis box up from the basement. They chortled fondly about all the excuses Hillary had provided them through high school for turning papers in late. Maeve gave Hillary credit for getting her into Cornell. Her application essay had been about her exotic sister. Its title had been a quote from Anaïs Nin: "I want to shout your imperfections!" But for all these idle bemusements, the dread remained, especially of a disaster in public, and Hillary still held the power to create a bathos of tears. For Maeve there was a familiar emotional cycle that in later life had become merely exhausting: embarrassment, guilt, apology, anger, guilt over anger. Some habits die hard. Once, post-transplant, at the dinner table, I found myself scolding Maeve for becoming distracted and not feeding Hillary.

"Dad," she said with a twinkle, "Hillary doesn't always have to come first." There was a pause, and then we all roared with laughter.

For Hillary's twenty-first birthday, we were determined to surpass the raucousness even of her eighteenth birthday party. This time we were not celebrating the mere fact of her survival, but the miracle of her operation and the glory of her transformation. We designed a proper send-off. The usual army of fans were invited: her teachers and doctors and nurses and caregivers—all her Annie Sullivans, most especially the amazing Helen Weisel—as well as our support group of family and close friends. This time, we added her babysitters from the darkest days of the mid-1980s, gorgeous high-school girls who had grown up to acquire their own children and PhDs. The flashiest of them, Amy Sabel, had become a Hollywood agent. We added the contingent of brilliant doctors at NIH, Alan Guttmacher and Donna Krasnewich, who had led us through the fascinating but ultimately fruitless search for a diagnosis on the human genome map. We longed for Dr. Boerkoel in Houston, Dr. Capecchi in Salt Lake City, and the contingent of Iowa doctors to be there as well.

For this blowout we rented our favorite neighborhood bistro, Arucola, where the pasta and pizza are heavenly, and the cute Italian waiters pamper and flirt with Hillary. When we proposed the idea to the manager, he said, "We have always been honored to have Hillary here."

Honored? I could only think of the flying silverware and broken glasses over the years as Hillary sat amid mayhem, the picture of innocence, like some Charles Addams character. His remark made me think that we should also have invited her fans among the local shopkeepers: the barber, the shoemaker, the drugstore owner, the Japanese fishmonger, the seamstress at Lads and Lassies, and the baker whose eyes always lit up when Hillary waddled in like E.T. And I imagined others who should be here: the chemist from D. R. Harris in London, Molly Mustard, and Hillary's Tuscan grape stomper from her bedroom poster.

And a blowout it was. Maeve had assembled a montage of pictures around the title "21 Years." The display was unforgiving, and included puffy China doll images of her when her nephrotic syndrome bloated her grotesquely. In turn, her clever nephrologist, Dr. Glenn Bock, had taken the cover of my book on the Third Crusade and altered it on the computer, replacing the face of Richard the Lionheart with my own, and Saladin's with Denise's, and altering the title to read *Worriers of God: James the Organ Seeker and Denise in the Kidney Crusade.* A tiny picture of Hilly in a tiara appeared in the embroidery of the book's spine.

Dr. Joan Conry stopped by early, looking radiant, on her way to the ballet. In her happiness for Hillary and for us, she remarked once again on the astounding fact that Denise and I were still married. So many parents of the ill children she treated had split. We had beaten the odds. Perhaps we weren't so bad at craps after all.

Among this eclectic group of celebrants Hillary sat, sassy and glowing, dressed in a grown-up purple ensemble that included a floor-length dress and a white feather boa. (While she was dressing, I'd had to block her from flushing the boa down the toilet.) Amid the clatter of glass and dishes and lively conversation, we moved her from table to table in the course of this three-hour feast so that everyone could have a chance to visit with her. Her presents were piled high on a side table. In her card one giver had written, "Hills, you have made me a better person."

Midway through the event, Denise rose to toast the assemblage, for they were all special people. But she singled out only a few: her two elder children, Maeve and Devin, "for this was not the life I would have wished for you," and her mother, Eileen, now eighty-five, who had been for eighteen years the very soul of Catholic charity. By the by, she also mentioned her husband, that New Age guy, whom she loved because he always cried at *Gone With the Wind,* no matter how many times he saw it. She might have mentioned the movie *E.T.,* because watching that with Hillary at Halloween had become a family tradition, and we could all relate to that.

I, too, gave a toast . . . for all the prodigious love that had been lavished on this child, and just as important, all the love that she had inspired in others. When that time came at the Pearly Gates, Hillary would do very well, I thought.

And then I read a parable. It had been written by a Greek Cypriot writer named Emy Markides, and sent to me only a few days earlier by a mutual friend in Cyprus. I put the title "Parable of the Two Pots" on it. It is the story of a water bearer in India who for two years had hauled water from a well in two pots. But one was cracked and had leaked water and was ashamed of its imperfection. Finally, the imperfect pot apologized to its bearer.

"Because of my flaws, you have to do all this work, and you don't get full value from your efforts," the pot said.

And the bearer answered, "Did you notice that there are flowers only on your side of the path, but not on the other pot's side? I have always known about your flaw, and I planted flower seeds on your side of the path. Every day while we walk back you've watered them. For two years I have been able to pick these beautiful flowers to decorate the table. Without you being just way you are, there would not be this beauty to grace the house."

Hours later, after darkness had descended and we were back home in our cups, an obscene black stretch limo pulled slowly up to our door. The window rolled down, and there was the cheery face of Hillary's pal, Helen Weisel.

"C'mon, girl," she called out to Hillary. "Let's go paint the town."

ACKNOWLEDGMENTS

Fragile Innocence has been six years in the making. In 2000 I prevailed on my wife, Denise Leary, to begin talking about our life with Hillary, knowing that the process of reopening those careworn boxes, long since closed, would be difficult for her. Without her superb memory, the expression of her profound love, and her willingness to cooperate, I knew I would not be able to tell Hillary's story. At first, we talked only once a week. I was disciplined about ending the conversations after twenty minutes. This is, therefore, Denise's book as much as it is Hillary's or mine.

After about a year, I laid the project aside. Our wait for a kidney transplant had stretched on and on into its eighth year. Without a transplant, without a diagnosis, there was no resolution to the story. But after the miraculous six weeks in Iowa during the summer of 2002, I felt that I could finish. It took me another three years of occasional and fitful writing to do so. In the finishing, my elder two children, Maeve and Devin, were distant enough in age at last to view their own experience with some dispassion, and they contributed importantly to the work.

In the book's final stages, I had help from stalwart friends and careful readers. Susan Kilborn, Jody Reston, Peter Kilborn, Lindsay Collins, and Maryssa Gilbride read early drafts. Dr. Alan Guttmacher at the National Institutes of Health (NIH) read the book for medical accuracy. Dr. Paul Peebles, Dr. Glenn Bock, and Dr. Joan Conry, the critical doctors in Hillary's care over the years, also weighed in with their memories and expertise. My superb agent, Joe Regal, always asked the right questions as I lurched forward and encouraged me to be patient and calm, until Hillary's odyssey achieved its natural completion.

I want to thank my editors, Shaye Areheart and Kim Kanner Meisner, for their enthusiasm, wisdom, and care.

And most of all, I want to thank Hillary.

ABOUT THE AUTHOR

JAMES RESTON, Jr., is the author of thirteen books, three plays, and numerous articles in national magazines, including *The New Yorker, Vanity Fair, Time, The New York Times Magazine, Esquire,* and *Rolling Stone.* He is a winner of the Prix Italia and the Dupont-Columbia Award for his 1983 National Public Radio documentary, "Father Cares: The Last of Jonestown." His last three books, *Galileo: A Life, The Last Apocalypse,* and *Warriors of God,* have been translated into ten foreign languages. *Warriors of God* and *Collision at Home Plate* have been optioned by Hollywood.

He received a Morehead Scholarship to attend the University of North Carolina, where he majored in philosophy and was an All South soccer player. After forty-two years, he still holds the single-game scoring record for the university. He attended Oxford University for his junior year. He has been a fellow at the American Academy in Rome and a scholar-in-residence at the Library of Congress. He was the *Newsweek,* PBS, and BBC candidate to be the first writer on the NASA space shuttle. He is currently a senior scholar at the Woodrow Wilson International Center for Scholars in Washington, D.C.